1800

HELL WITHOUT FIRE

HELL WITHOUT FIRE

CONVERSION IN SLAVE RELIGION

Love Henry Whelchel Jr.

ABINGDON PRESS/NASHVILLE

HELL WITHOUT FIRE
CONVERSION IN SLAVE RELIGION

Copyright © 2002 by Abingdon Press

This book is printed on recycled, acid-free, elemental-chlorine–free paper.

Library of Congress Cataloging-in-Publication Data

Whelchel, L. H.(Love Henry)
  Hell without fire : conversion in slave religion / Love Henry Whelchel Jr.
    p. cm.
Includes bibliographical references and index.
  ISBN 0-687-05283-1 (alk. paper)
    1. Afro-Americans—Religion. 2. Conversion—Christianity—History. 3. Colored Methodist Episcopal Church—History. 4. United States—Church history. I. Title.

  BR563.N4 W485 2002
  248.2'46'08996073—dc21

                                                              2001006907

All scripture quotations unless noted otherwise are taken from the *New Revised Standard Version of the Bible,* copyrighted © 1989, by the Division of Christian Education of the National Council of the Churches of Christ in the United States of America. Used by permission. All rights reserved.

Scriptures quotations marked (CEV) are from the *Contemporary English Version,* © 1991, 1992, 1995 by American Bible Society. Used by permission.

02 03 04 05 06 07 08 09 10 11—10 9 8 7 6 5 4 3 2 1

MANUFACTURED IN THE UNITED STATES OF AMERICA

In loving memory of

Love Henry Whelchel Sr.
Stuart C. Henry
C. Eric Lincoln

CONTENTS

ACKNOWLEDGMENTS

In some minute way, I hope this book will serve as a modest installment on the debt I owe to my devoted parents, lovely wife, wonderful children, faithful congregations, inquisitive students, and caring colleagues. Endless thanks to my wife, Larma, and my four young adult children—April, Kenyatta, Noel, and Love III—who have consistently supported my dreams and aspirations.

I would be remiss not to express my gratitude to the scholarly community at Clark Atlanta University, including: President Thomas W. Cole Jr., who gave me employment; Ms. Gwendolyn Donaway, my Administrative Assistant; Ms. Barbara DeVan, for her technical assistance; and faculty colleagues, Dr. Earle D. Clowney and Dr. Josephine Bradley, who were kind enough to read my manuscript and make insightful suggestions to enhance my work.

Finally, it is with an abundance of joy that I send this book out into the world with the hope that the readers will receive as much satisfaction as I did from writing the book.

L. Henry Whelchel
Spring 2002

INTRODUCTION

Seldom in world history has a people been so systematically disconnected and separated as African Americans. The institution of slavery was designed to separate Africans from their families, ancestors, language, name, history, beliefs, practices, and every attribute that contributed to their humanity. One writer describes this process of Africans' separation from their religion and homeland as a spiritual and cultural holocaust.[1] Religious conversion and training consequently were important because they gave slaves the resiliency to endure the systematic suppression of their beliefs and practices.

The title of this book, *Hell Without Fire*, is derived from an unnamed former slave's account of the reality of slavery. She was converted as she was returning from a spring and carrying a bucket of water on her head and two buckets in her hands. When she came to the door of the "big house," she encountered a ghost that she described as looking like Mars' Bill, a slave who had been dead for more than a year. The ghost appeared leaning against the side of the door with a red handkerchief around his neck and his legs crossed. She went up to him and said, "Mars' Bill," but he did not respond; he just stood looking up the hill as he did every day when he called the hogs. She stooped under his arm to go into the house. When she entered the house, her mistress asked in a scornful tone, "Who was that you talking to? Hush, you black liar. I heard you calling Mars' Bill." With that, the mistress struck the slave and beat her almost to death.[2]

While slavery had systematically denied this slave's status and identity as a person, the encounter with the ghost resulted in a new birth and a new freedom from her sense of worthlessness and from her captivity. The encounter initiated her delivery from her hell without fire. For the first time, the slave had a fixed point of certainty, purpose, and fulfillment. And because she realized that her prospects of learning to read were not promising she prayed this conversion prayer:

> I can't read a line either of the Scriptures or any other kind of writing, but I do know this: Whenever the truth from heaven is read before me I can talk to the Father. I often wish I did know how to read, but since I didn't have the chance to learn . . . being fearsome to be seen with a book when I was a slave . . . God has seen my need and made me satisfied. He has taken me—a fool—and hidden with me the secret of eternal life.[3]

CONVERSION

The conversion phenomenon—a change in one's religious life, whether the result of a sudden experience of God's grace or the gradual result of religious education and training—is not confined to any one race or section of the population, or even to any one period of history. Whether the converted is black or white, a slave or free, the common ground for all converted is this: We are all guilty of sin. In many American religious traditions, there is the motif of the need for universal conversion. The need for conversion also occurs cross-culturally in Christianity. Some religious groups emphasize a gradual process of salvation or conversion, which may include instruction, worship, and sacraments. Other evangelical groups emphasize conversion as a powerful and sudden experience of God's transforming grace. Still other groups, particularly those with Anglican roots, have combined elements from both traditions.

As the above summary demonstrates, we cannot generalize the conversion experience of any generation or in any part of the world. We must take into account the different cultural and institutional situations that shape patterns, norms, and forms of the individual expression of the spiritual conversion. However, the conversion of the slaves was necessarily different from that of the slaveholders. Because of the contrasting situations of the slaves and slaveholders and because of the slaves' spiritual need for more than they had, the conversion experience was much more radical for the slaves than for the slaveholders. Many whites sought fellowship with Christ and forgiveness for personal sins, but their conversion experience did not change societal ills, such as the institution of slavery. In fact, nothing was fundamentally at stake for the slaveholders.[4] This wasn't true for slaves because they were looking for a way to be freed from their captivity, even if it was only a spiritual freedom. European Americans wanted to be Christians, but they continued observing racial inequality. They wanted a new relationship with Christ but not with their neighbors, if those neighbors were black.

HELL AS MOTIVATOR FOR CHANGE

From early colonial times, European-American evangelists used the concept of hell to motivate the sinners' hunger for salvation and to urge conversion. Hell as the punishment for the unconverted sinner has roots in the ethos of American Christianity, as in the book of Revelation, and in literature, as in Dante's *Inferno* and John Milton's *Paradise Lost*. This terrifying motivator is again illustrated in Jonathan Edwards's famous sermon "Sinners in the Hands of an Angry God":

> That world of misery, that lake of burning brimstone, is extended abroad under you. There is the dreadful pit of the glowing flames of the wrath of God; there is hell's wide gaping mouth open; and you have nothing to stand upon, nor any thing to take hold of. There is nothing between you and hell but the air. . . . O sinner! consider the fearful danger you are in: it is a great furnace of wrath, a wide and bottomless pit, full of the fire of wrath, that you are held over in the hand of that God, whose wrath is provoked and incensed as much against you, as against many of the damned in hell.[5]

Such motivating sermons were reinforced by prayers such as the one prayed by an anonymous black woman for the seekers on the mourner's bench:

> O Father Almighty, O sweet Jesus, most gloried King, will you be so pleased to come dis way and put you eye on dese poor

13

mourners? O sweet Jesus, ain't you the Daniel God? Didn't you deliber de tree [three] chillun from the fiery furnis? Didn't you heah [hear] Jonah cry in de belly ub de whale? O, if dere be one seekin' mourner here dis afternoon, if dere be one sinkin' Peter, if dere be one weepin' Mary, if dere be one doubtin' Thomas, won't you be pleased to come and deliber 'em? Won't you mount your Gospel hoss, an' ride roun' de souls of dese yere mourners, and say, "Go in peace and sin no moah?" Don't you be so pleased to come wid de love in one han' and de fan in de odder han', to fan away doubts? Won't you be so pleased to shake dese here souls over hell, an' not let 'em fall in! [Amen.][6]

Edwards's sermon and the woman's prayer exemplify what slaves and free people thought about converting to Christianity: Christian conversion was a choice between spending eternity in heaven or in hell.

However, the hell presented in the slaves' conversion narratives is not just a place in the afterlife. Hell was a metaphor for their present situation. The slaves viewed their plight as a hell on earth, which provided the context and motivation for their conversion and transformation. This hell without fire, in the context of conversion, became a purifying process. Conversion was viewed as a means of transformation and transportation from the realm of debased and degraded slaves into the realm of a chosen people. In other words and in relation to the Bible, the slaves were like the poor man Lazarus, and the slave masters were the rich man who would not care for Lazarus; the slaves expected a reversal of fortunes in the end (Luke 16:19-21).

The conversion experience (as a result of a sudden experience of God's grace) often was expressed as the death of the old carnal life and the "new birth" of a spiritual life. Baptism was a symbol of death with the immersion of the flesh under the water and of a spiritual rebirth as the converts came from under the water—often with visible emotion.

After seeing hell, heaven, and God in a vision, Nancy Williams, a slave in Virginia, recounted that she started shouting in the spirit and never stopped.[7] She says, "I died the sinner death and ain't got to die no more."[8] The slave was called by name in baptism and then "was killed dead to sin and made alive again in Jesus Christ."[9] Nancy described her struggle for, and vision of, salvation as a journey down to the fires of hell and then up to the glory of heaven, an eternal home not made with hands. Blacks were not the only converted to express such emotion. White people frequently were baptized with blacks and also "'came through' shouting and singing at the same time."[10]

Because slaves were homeless and without family ties on either side of the Atlantic, they looked to God for a place they could call home. As Nancy Williams said, slaves were looking forward to their new home not made with human hands. Heaven was this home and the place they could reunite with long-separated family. The slaves sang "I'm going there to see my mother'n, father'n [and family]."[11] And they in fact did visit departed family from time to time in trances and visions, much like the vision of the young slave girl who believed she saw a dead Mars' Bill waiting by the door as if he were still alive. After the slaves were converted, they often believed that they had overcome sin and death. The new birth validated them to live as long as God wanted them to live and prepared for them a home not made with hands.

The term "new birth" describes the conversion experiences of African Americans and European Americans. The institutionalization of slavery dictated a more radical new birth for the slaves than for the slaveholders. The sins from which the slaves sought deliverance were more than card playing, drinking, and fiddling. Slaves wanted cleansing and a concomitant rebirth. Their cleansing and new birth was a holistic experience that saved the converts from corporate and personal sins. The conversion experience often was in the form of a metaphorical stroke of lightning that would strike at the crown of the head but could be felt to the soles of the feet, thereby marking its total cleansing of the converted. Conversion was crucial for slaves because it provided them a sense of worth and identity while separated from loved ones. Also, it was crucial for the slaves to have a personal God who identified and empathized with their unique struggles.

Moreover, the transformation that accompanied the conversion also enabled slaves to express a moral superiority over their masters. Yolanda Pierce, in her insightful essay "How Saul Became

Paul: The African-American Conversion Experience," retells the story of a former slave named Charlie who met his former master after the Civil War. Charlie had been unmercifully beaten by his master and bore lacerations on his back as evidence of this abuse. When asked by his former master if Charlie had forgiven him, Charlie revealed that he indeed had forgiven his former master:

> For the God I serve is a God of love and I can't go to his kingdom with hate in my heart. I have felt the power of God and tasted his love and this has killed all the spirit of hate in my heart. . . . Whenever a man has been killed dead and made alive in Christ Jesus, he no longer feels like he did when he was a servant of the devil.[12]

Slaves and slaveholders arrived at the point of conversion with different hopes and agendas. Nevertheless, they influenced one another's beliefs and practices because they frequently were converted under the same roof and by the same evangelist. As slaveholders may have been influenced by the demonstrative and spontaneous worship style of the slaves, it is likely that slaves were influenced by the slaveholders' focus on personal salvation, which embraced virtues such as honesty, chastity, and humility. In short, slaves and slaveholders could have come to the conclusion—had they been afforded the opportunity to examine their situations critically and theologically—that one thing they had in common was the need for deliverance.

Concluding that the conversion experience brought together slaves and slaveholders may sound contrived for the purpose of this book, but it is in fact true that the two groups were brought together. Not only did they come together in a physical space to hear a single evangelist, but also they inspired and influenced each other's culture and religious practices. We recognize that the dominant European culture had immense influence on black religion. For example, the majority of African Americans today are members of European-founded, mainline Protestant denominations. But often we fail to account fully for the influence of African Americans on European Americans. For example, the Church of God in Christ, a mainline Protestant denomination, was founded by an African American.

This coalescence of Western and African religious cultures was not the only interrelation of slaves and masters. Slaves often lived in the same houses as their masters. When they did live separately, the house structures were often similar. Slaves and masters did much of the same work, often together, and shared their churches and their God. In spite of the inevitable interpenetrating of cultures, white masters usually appeared unaware of their own change in the process. Nevertheless, the African influence on ecstatic religious experience, spirit possession, healing, understanding of the Holy Spirit, honoring the spirit of the dead, and even a renewed emphasis on the cyclical concept of time, was deep and far reaching for all American religious experiences.[13]

As Peter H. Wood maintains in the essay entitled "Jesus Christ Has Got Thee at Last," most students of American intellectual and religious history are aware of Benjamin Franklin's encounter with the famous evangelist George Whitefield. But very few are familiar with John Marrant, a free black man, who was one of Whitefield's most celebrated converts. Marrant was converted during Whitefield's final visit to the South in 1769. Marrant was born in New York in 1755 and moved to Charleston, South Carolina, during his boyhood. He was innately gifted in music and earned money by performing for white patrons. At the age of fourteen, while en route to an engagement and with his horn wrapped around one arm, Marrant passed a house where an evangelical service was in session and heard what he described as "a crazy man" who was "hollering." A man standing outside the meetinghouse informed Marrant that the crazy man was the evangelist Whitefield. The man challenged Marrant to go inside and "blow the French horn among them." Marrant later recalled that he "liked the proposal well enough,"

> but expressed my fears of being beaten for disturbing them; but upon his promising to stand by and defend me, I agreed. So, we went and with much difficulty got within the doors. I was pushing the people to make room, to get the horn off my shoulder to blow it, just as Mr. Whitefield was naming his text, and looking around, and as I thought, directly upon me, and pointing with his finger, he uttered these words, "PREPARE TO MEET THY GOD, O, ISRAEL." The

Lord accompanied the word with such power, that I was struck to the ground, and lay both speechless and senseless nearly half an hour.[14]

Young Marrant had a sudden conversion, and he was taken from the hall delirious and "hollering." But when the meeting adjourned, "Mr. Whitefield came into the vestry and being told of my condition, he came immediately, and the first word he said to me was, 'Jesus Christ has got thee at last.'"[15]

The great revivalists—Whitefield, Robert Williams, and Samuel Davies—all welcomed the energy and enthusiasm blacks contributed to the success of their meetings. Reverend Samuel Davies, a successful Presbyterian revivalist, remarked in 1757 that blacks had a confused hunger for the good news: "Many of them only seem to desire to be, they know not what: They feel themselves uneasy in their present condition, and therefore, desire change."[16] They desired change, recognized the spirit and spirit power, and were ready to participate with fervor and enthusiasm in ceremonies of rebirth and spiritual renewal.

The insatiable hunger of African Americans for the gospel captured the attention of George Whitefield. His relation to slavery was ambiguous: He never denounced the institution of slavery, but he did admonish slave owners to practice civility in the treatment of their slaves and to recognize the common need for black and white, slave and free, to be delivered from sin. "Think you, [your children] are any way better by nature, than the poor negroes!" Whitefield wrote in "A Letter to the Inhabitants of Maryland, Virginia, North and South Carolina." He continues:

> No, in nowise! Blacks are just as much, and no more, conceived and born in sin, as white men are; both, if born and bred up here, I am persuaded are naturally capable of the same improvement. And as for the grown negroes, I am apt to think, whenever the gospel is preached with power among them, that many will be brought effectually home to God.[17]

As a leader of the Great Awakening, Whitefield was able to influence Africans through his revival sermons by speaking of the spiritual change that God provided and that they desired.

THE ROAD AHEAD

The first chapter, "Context for Conversion: Atlantic Slave Trade to the First Great Awakening" examines the role of conversion as the pretext for the slave trade, which led in turn to a moral dilemma for the Christian nations attempting to defend their involvement in human bondage. Their use of conversionist language in defense of slavery precipitated other moral and economic problems. After slaves were converted and baptized, questions arose about their status—would they still be slaves or would they be free? There was an old English law that forbade Christian believers to hold other believers in bondage. If this law had been applied, it would have jeopardized the slave property of the slaveholders. The purpose of this chapter is to examine the various ways the language of conversion was used to interpret and analyze, in a Christian context, the dilemmas of slave religion.

The second chapter, "Conversion and Religious Training: Religion with Letters [1700–1799]," focuses on the ways conversionist language was used by religious and civil authorities in seeking support and permission from slaveholders to evangelize their slaves. The religious training of slaves in the eighteenth century, initiated by the Anglican denomination, embraced "religion with letters," which included teaching the slaves to read and write. Since literacy was an integral part of conversion for the Anglican Church, the religious training of slaves became a primary concern in helping Africans' participation in the liturgy and worship. The chapter also examines how the conversion motif initiated the enterprise of education, enabling blacks to emerge from slavery with their own churches, ministers, teachers, colleges, and institutions.

The third chapter, "Conversion and the Plantation Missions: Religion Without Letters [1800–1865]," discovers how preachers crafted a conversionist appeal compatible with the political and religious climate of the nineteenth century, which prohibited slave converts from learning to read and write. This adaptation of conversionist rhetoric was adopted in response to the sporadic slave insurrections, abolitionist propaganda, and the humanitarian impulse of the Second Great Awakening. The emergence of plantation missions, sponsored by mainline southern denominations, was designed to implement the oral method of religious training to counter attacks on the institution of slavery by those who advocated social reform.

Chapter 4, "Conversion and the Formation of the Colored Methodist Episcopal Church [1866–1870]," examines the usage of conversionist language in the formation of the Colored Methodist Episcopal Church during the postemancipation era. While the North defeated the South in the Civil War, northerners neither won the loyalty of the South nor changed attitudes toward slavery or toward African Americans. Consequently, southern Methodists continued their use of conversionist motifs from the antebellum era in order to maintain control over, and influence of, their former slaves in the postbellum South. This chapter provides a close look at the conversionist strategy used by the white northern Methodists, northern African Methodists, and white southern Methodists to compete for the more than 70,000 souls that remained with the Southern Methodist Missions. To keep from losing complete control and to avoid further defection of their African members, the southern Methodists reluctantly consented to participating in the organizing of an independent black Methodist denomination in the south and consequently retained a paternalistic relationship with black Methodists throughout the postemancipation era.

Instead of focusing only on African-American religious experience, which has been the traditional approach to conversion and slavery, this study examines the intercontinental influences and the interaction, or intimacy, of European-American and African-American cultural and religious experience. Readers trained in the field of religion may not find an abundance of new data on the subject but will discern a variety of ways the conversion nuances are used to analyze and interpret the black religious experience. As advanced students of African-American religious history will quickly recognize, this book is intended, not to break new ground as original scholarship, but to provide students a useful summary of the corpus of literature on the African-American religious experience.

Excellent analyses of that experience have appeared in the scholarly texts listed below and should be used for additional study:

Berlin, Ira. *Many Thousands Gone: The First Two Centuries of Slavery in North America.* Cambridge, Mass.: Belknap Press of Harvard University Press, 1998.

Coleman, Will. *Tribal Talk: Black Theology, Hermeneutics, and African/American Ways of "Telling the Story."* University Park, Pa.: Pennsylvania State University Press, 1998.

Earl, Riggins. *Dark Symbols, Obscure Signs: God, Self, and the Slave Mind.* Maryknoll, N.Y.: Orbis Books, 1993.

Elkins, Stanley M. *Slavery: A Problem in American Institutional and Intellectual Life,* 3rd ed. Chicago: University of Chicago Press, 1976.

Frey, Sylvia R., and Betty Wood. *Come Shouting to Zion: African American Protestantism in the American South and British Caribbean to 1830.* Chapel Hill, N.C.: University of North Carolina Press, 1998.

Grant, Jacquelyn. *White Women's Christ, Black Women's Jesus.* Atlanta: Scholars Press, 1989.

Harrison, William Pope. *The Gospel among the Slaves.* Nashville: Publishing House of the MEC, 1893.

Hopkins, Dwight N. *Down, Up, and Over: Slave Religion and Black Theology.* Minneapolis: Fortress Press, 2000.

Lincoln, C. Eric, and Lawrence H. Mamiya. *The Black Church in the African American Experience.* Durham, N.C.: Duke University Press, 1990.

Long, Charles H. *Significations: Signs, Symbols, and Images in the Interpretation of Religion.* Aurora, Colo.: Davies Group, 1999.

Martin, Sandy D. *Black Baptists and African Missions: The Origins of a Movement, 1880–1915.* Macon, Ga.: Mercer University Press, 1989.

Murphy, Larry G. *Down by the Riverside: Readings in African American Religion.* New York: New York University Press, 2000.

Raboteau, Albert J. *Canaan Land: A Religious History of African Americans.* New York: Oxford University Press, 2001.

————. *Slave Religion: The "Invisible Institution" in the Antebellum South.* New York: Oxford University Press, 1978.

Sobel, Mechal. *Trabelin' On: The Slave Journal to an Afro-Baptist Faith.* Princeton, N.J.: Princeton University Press, 1988.

Washington, James. *Frustrated Fellowship: The Black Baptist Quest for Social Power.* Macon, Ga.: Mercer University Press, 1986.

Wilmore, Gayraud S. *Black Religion and Black Radicalism: An Interpretation of the Religious History of African Americans,* 3rd ed. Maryknoll, N.Y.: Orbis Books, 1998.

The above scholars and others have provided the background of the analysis and the context for the short history that follows. This book will make a significant contribution to the above books by examining the conversionist appeals that created a context for intimacy and interaction and that provided an opportunity for blacks and whites to share their religious and cultural heritages—in fact to create a culture in common. This book presents a synthesis of scholarship on the seldom-studied topic of slave conversion, using the conversionist language to produce a unified interpretation of slave religion and colonial Christianity. It highlights the African- and European-Americans' powerful influence in shaping each other's culture and religion.

In contrast to the traditional topical approach, the focus of this book is on examining the role of conversion in the rise of the black religious experience from slavery through the emergence of the institutional life of the Christian Methodist Episcopal denomination. Until recently, historians have ignored the conversion of African Americans to Christianity during the colonial period. There has been a tendency of scholars to focus primarily on the nineteenth and twentieth centuries, a time for which the resources are less limited and blacks are more readily recognized as part of the mainstream of American Christianity. In addition, there has been an oversimplification of the conversion process, in which scholars ignore the impact the rhetoric of conversion had on promoting slavery and shaping colonial Christianity.

CHAPTER ONE

Context for Conversion: Atlantic Slave Trade to the First Great Awakening

The European slave trade is rooted deeply in the city of Benin in Guinea, which is on the West Coast of Africa. Benin was the capital of Guinea and was rich in natural resources and its population highly civilized. It was noted for its striking beauty, with shade trees lining the streets and homes made of red clay polished to such a high gloss that explorers took them to be made of red marble.[1] The first white man to arrive in Benin was Ruy de Sequeira, and he arrived in 1472. He paid homage to King Oba by prostrating himself before the king. By doing so, he won the favor of the king and received permission to trade for ivory, gold dust, and slaves. Oba was subsequently introduced to Christianity and was sympathetic toward the Christian faith. However, Oba was not able to convert without losing his office because Benin was a theocracy ruled by traditional African religion.

In 1495, Haitians enslaved in the West Indies rebelled against the Spanish missionaries who had subjected them to hard labor and showed disregard for their culture and beliefs. Charles IV, the king of Spain, responded by sending Christopher Columbus and his infantry back to the island, only three years after his initial visit, to quell the revolt. In the process, the native Americans were brutally massacred. The unmerciful extermination of the native Americans won the sympathy of the Spanish courtier Bartholomew de las Casas, who appealed to Charles IV on behalf of the native Americans survivors.[2]

He proposed to replace native Americans with Africans as slaves to work the West Indian plantations and mines. Charles responded favorably to the request and granted permission to ship four thousand Africans to the West Indian colonies. The Spanish not only initiated this slave trade to the West Indies but also continued to control the market by issuing the Asiento import license. At the outset of the Spanish slave trade, it was unchristian and illegal for an individual to hold another individual in bondage. To circumvent the legal and moral impediments, traders were required to secure special permission from the King of Spain. The license (or contract) the crown issued that allowed slaves to be brought into the Spanish colonies was this Asiento. After the slave traders had been licensed, they were required to pay tax to the crown on each slave brought into the colony, which enhanced the diplomatic and economic influence of the king at home and abroad. In 1518, las Casas sold the Asiento to a Genoese merchant, who then, in Lisbon, loaded a cargo of slaves shipped from Guinea.[3]

During the last decade of the fifteenth century, the Portuguese had begun to explore the coast of Guinea and Cape of Good Hope, and they began claiming exclusive rights to the whole African continent. The Portuguese also built Port Elimina, the first slaveholding depot on the Gold Coast. The African king Kwame Assa welcomed Portuguese trading in the country but was reluctant to allow the white man to build a fort. The African king politely discouraged the building of a fortified trading post:

> I am not insensible to the high honor which you grate martes [your great master], the Chief of Portugal has this day conferred upon me. . . . It is far preferable that both our nations should continue on the same footing they have hitherto done, allowing ships to come and go as well.[4]

However, Portugal was determined to establish a permanent foothold in Africa. And it took eighty years for them to erect the Elimina Castle. The slave depot was elaborately equipped with high towers, cannons, and a dungeon capable of accommodating slaves.

It is ironic that the hope of converting enslaved Africans provided European Christian nations with a defense for the Atlantic slave trade. The countries involved in the slave trade—Portugal, Spain, the Netherlands, France, and England—defended slavery on the grounds that Africans must be converted from paganism and barbarism to Christianity and that the enslavement of Africans would be the best chance to convert them. The slave traders invoked God's blessings upon the slave ships that transported their human cargo and gave the ships "holy" names such as *Brotherhood, Charity, Gift of God, Morning Star,* and *Jesus.*[5]

The conquest and subsequent conversion of the African people contributed significantly to the promotion of these inane and inhuman atrocities. Under the guise of the universal need for salvation and the Europeans willing to bring that salvation, the institution of slavery was made to appear more palatable by enslaving bodies in order to save souls. It is widely recognized that the fifteenth-century Catholic Church granted its blessings for European princes to make war on the Saracens and other so-called infidels to spread the Christian faith.[6] Less recognized is that it was fairly common practice during the age of exploration for European kings and queens to grant commercial companies the right to engage in the slave trade under the pretense of promoting Christianity.[7] Slavers as well as kings assuaged their guilt by "emphasizing the grace of faith [was] made available to Africans, who otherwise would die as pagans."[8]

Conversion to Christianity played several key, sometimes conflicting, roles in the emerging slave trade. At the beginning of the slave trade in Benin, King John II of Portugal did not send missionaries to the Africans, but he did send a message to King Oba encouraging him to lead his subjects away from their traditional African religions, which he described as "heresies, gross idolatry, and fetishes."[9] With the expansion of the European slave trade, African rulers saw Christianity as economically attractive, a means to gain wealth rather than spiritual power. By cultivating their emergent friendship with the Europeans—even by converting to Christianity—some Africans were able to exchange fellow human beings for gifts and ammunition.[10] The slave traders and missionaries often supported and cooperated with each other in their work. They usually operated in the same geographic regions, and there emerged a fusion of economic and spiritual aspirations as Europeans competed for both souls and bodies. Conversion became necessary for European control of the area. The slave traders ensured little opposition to conversion by reminding tribal rulers that "baptism would bring [the Africans] guns and grace."[11] A clear example of the tangible rewards for converting to Christianity is given in a letter from the king of Portugal to the ruler of Benin:

> Therefore, with a very good will we send you the clergy that you have asked for; they bring with them all the things that are needed to construct you and your people in the knowledge of our faith. And we trust in our Lord that He will bestow His grace upon you, that you may confess it and be saved by it—for all the things of the world pass away, and those of the other last forever. For when we see that you have embraced the teaching of Christianity, there will be nothing in our realm with which we shall not be made to favour you, whether it be arms or cannon and all other weapons of war for use against your enemies; of such things we have a great store.[12]

The Europeans contributed to a decline in African culture and civilization by encouraging intertribal strife, by providing ammunition for Africans to engage in civil warfare, by promoting the slave trade through indirect military pressure (controlling the guns and horses that were vital to the military success of the African nations), and by providing rival African rulers with musket power. Africans were enticed to trade black gold for ammunition in order to engage in war with their neighbors. Thus emerged a cycle: Success in war guaranteed a large supply of slaves (captured during the war) to pay the Europeans for their military technology, which was needed for success in war. The need for guns and horses forced African leaders to seek more slaves for their own political and economic success.[13] As argued elsewhere, prior to the arrival of Europeans, the west coast of Africa was far from "naked savagery."[14] There were thriving cities and towns inhabited by highly skilled artisans working in wood carving, agriculture, religions, government, and music.[15] A true history of Africa counters the myth that the enslavement of Africans was providential mercy delivered by contact with European civilization in America.

After the Spaniards had formally opened the slave trade to the New World, they were joined by the Dutch, Portuguese, French, and English. One of the earliest English slave gathering expeditions was headed by Sir John Hawkins. He departed from England in October 1562 and spent some time off the coast of Guinea, where he captured three hundred Africans and sold them to Spaniards.[16] The slave trade is recognized to have continued for a period of nearly four hundred years. Though Africans arrived in the New World almost at the same time that white colonists began to settle on the Island of Hispaniola or in Haiti in 1501, the slave trade is recognized to have begun formally with the first black cargo from Africa arriving in the West Indies in 1518. The slave trade was greatly restrained by 1865, but it did not officially end until 1880.[17] From arrival in America, Blacks were dehumanized and treated as material goods and articles or merchandise and property in the form of units of labor.

The selling of human beings involved a systematic process for capturing a potential slave. The European slave traders would establish contact with the tribal chief first, and the chief would appoint a *caboceer* responsible for traveling the countryside and capturing the Africans to be sold at the prices previously agreed upon between the trader and the African chief. The captives then were sold to slave traders in exchange for such commodities as brass utensils, ivory boxes of beads, gunpowder, guns, whiskey, brandy and rum, and a variety of other goods. African labor was thus commercialized as "black gold."[18]

After the Africans had been captured, they were held in a *baracoon*, a makeshift prison on the beach. This structure served as a holding pen in which the captives were treated like pigs, but only until European slave traders bought the human cargo for slave markets in the New World. In the *baracoon*, Africans were shaved clean and soaked in palm oil to disguise their ages and physical conditions. Often, European slave traders summoned their personal physicians to inspect prospective property, and those Africans who passed the physical were branded with a hot iron and packed in small cubicles on ships for the middle passage across the Atlantic. Most ships were overcrowded with Africans stacked into holes no deeper than eighteen inches and no longer and wider than a coffin, maximizing the profits. The atrocity of the six to ten week voyage across the Atlantic caused some Africans to go insane. Other Africans suffocated. In desperation, some killed fellow passengers for more living space. It was not uncommon, particularly with regard to the African slave men, to find a dead slave chained to a live one when the arduous voyage had ended.[19] The untold and unknown number of Africans cast overboard satisfied the hunger of sharks that might have followed ships, waiting for another African to be sent to an Atlantic grave.

However, it is a much-overlooked fact that slavery, even slavery of Africans, did not begin with the Europeans. In fact, the practice of slavery has existed in some form in every society since the dawn of history, and even in African society. To justify one form of slavery over another is absurd, but it is important to recognize that the practice of slavery in Africa was dramatically different from the practice of slavery in America and Europe. First and foremost, slavery in Africa was not the result of the stigma of color or race. In West Africa, some slaves were eligible for social mobility. They could become soldiers, counselors, and heads of state. They could obtain wealth. The stigma of slavery did not follow Africans perpetually in Africa as it did for Africans in America.[20] Second, African slaves were usually house servants and generally were not sold or transferred from one owner to another as goods. In fact, these domestic servants were granted the privilege of owning property, marrying, and sometimes becoming guardians of the masters' children. Even prisoners of war and imported slaves could not be sold.[21] Moreover, most men and women enslaved in West Africa were captured during inter-tribal warfare and were permitted to buy their freedom with goods or money.[22]

Masters who killed slaves generally received the same punishment as murderers of freemen received, which is a clear contrast to the legal status of slaves in America. African slaves also had a legal right to one day of rest and to one to three days each week, working for their own behalf, something unheard of in the annals of American slavery. Finally, African slaves enjoyed a more stable family life than New World slaves. For instance, if a man were sold into slavery, his wife accompanied him, but she kept her freedom. A wife who was also a slave could not be separated from her children, and her offspring were born free. Wives were protected from the sexual abuse of their masters. Masters who broke this rule could be fined, or their slaves could be set free.[23] In short, West African slaves had more rights and received better treatment than the slaves in America.

It is widely acknowledged that the slavery the Europeans eventually practiced was unprecedented in the annals of history. From 1518 to 1880, it is likely that more than 100 million Africans were either killed or transported from Africa.[24] This was the most drastic mass movement of human beings in history. Every African enslaved in America and all of his or her descendants were slaves for life. In the early 1700s, the southern colonies enacted laws that made freeing slaves considerably more difficult, compounding the tragedy. For a slave to receive manumission, or emancipation, the slave's master had to petition the legislature, post a bond (usually $500), and pay transportation out of the state for any freed slave.

Slave families had no legal protection or support. Masters could separate family members and sexually abuse slave women and children without fear of legal consequences. There were no provisions or standards in place to care for the clothing, housing, and feeding of slaves. The life of a slave was an extremely precarious existence in America. Whites who murdered blacks were seldom tried or convicted, and those who were convicted received light sentencing. Blacks were forbidden to testify against whites. It was suicidal for a black person to challenge a white person. For hitting a white person, slaves were often severely beaten or mutilated by castration or by the cutting off of an ear. And slave masters inflicted harsh punishment to discourage revolts and slaves from running away. Slaveholders considered it logical and fruitful to make examples of rebellious slaves by mutilating them. The planters valued neither the health nor the life of the slave too much because Africa provided a replenishment of slaves for free labor.[25]

The slave trade proved detrimental, even fatal, for both blacks and whites. Many Europeans directly involved in the slave trade died of malaria, dysentery, alcohol abuse, and gunshot wounds. As said earlier transported slaves were murdered by masters, killed on the ships by other slaves, and died from suffocation while being transported. There were no winners; all were losers. It made captives of the slaves as well as the slaveholders. But instead of suffering from physical bondage, slaveholders suffered from what the slave trader John Newton called "a numbness upon the heart" and "[indifference] to the sufferings of . . . fellow creatures." Another source says that the most distinguishing feature of slavery affected the traders: The horror was "not its dangers, not the loss of life, not even the cruelties it inflicted on millions, but rather the numbness of the traders and the loss of human sympathies."[26] In addition, the slave trade marked the genesis of a cultural captivity that has characterized American race relations for centuries.

The color of the African skin also figured heavily into the misconceptions and the conversionist appeal. The genesis of color consciousness originated, at least in part, with the Europeans' initial contact with Africans. What stood out most prominently from their first contact was the African skin color. Europeans often commented on the striking contrast between their white complexion and the dark pigmentation of the Africans. Other cultural and linguistic differences did not go unnoticed by the early explorers, but the most indelible impression was the African color.[27] The value placed on color perhaps led Europeans to conclude that all differences between them and the Africans—biological, social, cultural, linguistic, and so on—were based on color or race. Since skin color was such a domineering influence, some Europeans began to ask why Africans were black. They discussed at length the answers of the Greeks (and, for example, the work of Ptolemy), who believed that the Africans' pigmentation and wooly hair was due to exposure to the heat and sun.[28] They even extrapolated that people in the north were white due to the cold climate. In quest for answers, some turned to scripture and found the words of the prophet Jeremiah regarding differences of color. The Hebrew seer asked, "Can Ethiopians change their skin or leopards their spots?" (Jeremiah 13:23). The permanence of the Ethiopians' color also inspired Homer to describe them as "blameless." This implied to European commentators that Ethiopians should not be held responsible for their color and remote civilization.[29]

A THEOLOGICAL "CATCH-22": THE CONFLICTING MEANS AND ENDS OF SLAVERY

At the outset, the African slave trade met only slight opposition. What opposition existed immediately dwindled when it was stated that the slave trade was a means of converting heathens to Christianity. However, the excuse of enslaving Africans for religious motivation created unforeseen problems. The conversion and baptism of Africans compelled colonial American Christianity to face the question of the slaves' humanity. It was a long-standing English tradition that baptized persons should, according to the civil and church canon, be free. It was a widespread English belief that a common need for conversion leveled "all men before God as sinners in need of salvation."[30]

The old English custom that prohibited one Christian from holding another in bondage also had serious implications for those who owned slave property.[31] The colonial establishment was confronted with a theological dilemma. To deny the conversion and baptism of slaves would undermine the rationale for the slave trade, but to embrace manumission of slaves after their conversion and baptism would alienate the slaveholders who would lose their property. Consequently, we must attend carefully to the exact form of the conversion motif used by American slaveholders.

Initially, conversion justified Christians' involvement in slavery on the grounds that Africans needed to be converted and civilized. Once African slaves had become Christians, complicated moral

31

and economic problems emerged regarding their status. If the slaves were freed after baptism, then the slaveholders would lose their property. According to English law, baptism changes the status of Africans from slaves to freemen. Attempting to resolve this inherent conflict, the church claimed that Africans, already barbaric and heathen, had souls doomed to eternal perdition and destruction. Color thus became a stigma, an inherent inferiority that made Africans' true salvation impossible. Consequently, the baptism of African slaves was not sufficient reason for emancipation, and it did not remove their slave status.

In 1664, Maryland became the first colony to enact laws explicitly denying slaves freedom based on their conversion to Christianity.[32] Three years later, Virginia enacted a similar measure, which held that the freedom of a slave's soul did not apply to the body.[33] At first, the Virginia Assembly protected Africans who were Christians prior to coming to the New World as it protected white indentured servants. However, this law was repealed in 1682 and replaced with a measure that declared that conversion before or after importation did not alter the status of an African slave.[34] During the colonial period, Maryland, Virginia, the Carolinas, New York, and New Jersey eventually agreed that the saving of an African soul did not extricate his or her body from slave status.[35]

The colonial authorities used a particular language of conversion—differentiating salvation of the soul from salvation of the body—to give the institution of slavery a semblance of civility. Attempting to justify the evil of slavery, slaveholders separated the slave's soul from the body; freedom of the soul did not imply freedom for the body. The justification for separating an African's body and soul was the perception that the African's biological, social, cultural, and linguistic differences made it impossible for him or her to be treated as European Americans' equals. In short, the conversion motif—defined and domesticated as European Americans saw fit—met their economic and political needs and aided both the civil and the church authorities in addressing the moral dilemma: How could a Christian nation condone and contribute to the institution of slavery?

Despite their legitimation of the slave trade, slaveholders were attracted primarily to Africans for the free labor they provided, cultivating the vast natural resources discovered in the New World. Searching for an acceptable labor force was also the priority of Spain and England in the seventeenth century when the two countries began trading goods for slaves in Africa. It did not take long to recognize the inadequacies of captured Native Americans and European indentured servants meeting their labor needs. Native Americans proved an inadequate answer to European labor problems because of their perceived lack of stamina, lack of natural immunity to European diseases, and unwillingness to adopt the European culture. "They waste away," lamented Thorogood Moor, "and have done [so] ever since our first arrival among them (as they say themselves) like snow against the sun, so that very probably forty years hence there will scarce be an Indian seen in our America."[36] Likewise, white servants from Europe proved to be unsatisfactory, owing to insufficient numbers and the difficulty of identifying runaway white servants from free whites. Nevertheless, during the early colonial period, there was less distinction between indentured servants and black bondsmen. However, blacks did not have written indentures that stated their rights and limited time of service.

The physical and cultural differences provided a rationale for treating blacks with less respect than white indentured servants. And by the eighteenth century, color had become not only the evidence of slavery but also a badge of degradation, with color prejudice engraved into American custom and law.[37] Africans were an anomaly in the human race. Europeans would use the excuse of the Africans' skin color to justify the enslavement of them. They based their trade on the stigma of color, and the legacy of this color consciousness is imbedded in the fabric of European American society.

CONVERSION AS ANNIHILATION: PERPETRATING A CULTURAL HOLOCAUST

Unlike other ethnic groups in America, African Americans, now known for their religious and cultural diversity, were not allowed to integrate the memory of their ancestors and native religions overtly into their own lives. Stripped of their heritage, they were nearly dissolved as a people and lost almost all sense of identity, purpose, and calling. Forbidden to speak their native languages, to be identified by their African names, to practice their own customs and traditions, and to preserve their native beliefs and values, African Americans scarcely were able to give meaning to the humiliation and brutalities they endured daily. Slavery and the African cultural holocaust were attempts to deprive slaves of their creativity and resilience and to deny their sense of self. This contrasted sharply to the treatment that other immigrant peoples received as they entered the American "melting pot." Jon Butler, in his book *Awash in a Sea of Faith,* has noted this contrasting treatment of races in the New World:

> Whatever the difficulties and anomalies of colonization, a broad range of religiously inclined Europeans—Puritans, Scottish, Presbyterians, German Lutherans, Dutch Reformed, Quakers and Jews—not only survived in America but often eventually prospered both individually and spiritually. But the rich religious systems of Akan, Ashanti, Dahoman, Ibo and Yoruba societies—to name only some of the major sources of African religion in America—collapsed in the shattering cultural destructiveness of British slaveholding.[38]

Africans were some of the earliest immigrant arrivals in America, but the promise of freedom and new opportunities anticipated by European immigrants was not accorded to them. Stanley Elkins has compared the arriving Africans to concentration camp. victims, both groups traumatized by their arbitrary treatment within captivity and unable to sustain their psychological and cultural values.[39] Historian Richard Hofstadter embraced Elkins's thesis with a striking description of the implementation of the slave trade:

> To Africans, stunned by the long ordeal of the Middle Passage, the auctions could only have marked a decrescendo in fright and depression; . . . as one tries to imagine the mental state of the newly arrived Africans, one must think of people still sick, depleted and depressed by the ordeal of the voyage, the terror of the

34

unknown, the sight of the deaths and suicides, and the experience of total helplessness in the hands of others. What they had been and known receded rapidly, and the course of their experience tended to reduce their African identity to the withered husks of dead memories.[40]

Rarely recognized is the fact that white denominations offering instruction in Christianity contributed to the process of eradicating traditional African religion and culture. European Americans regarded African beliefs and practices, such as the veneration of ancestors, drumming, ceremonial dancing, spirit possession, and shouting, not only as expressions of the kind of paganism they claimed to deplore but also as vestiges of an identity they felt they needed to destroy in order to enhance their control over their slaves. For more than three centuries, African-American slaves were not only denied the freedom of their bodies but also robbed of their history, heritage, and most important, their humanity. E. Franklin Frazier, who represents an extreme viewpoint of the lack of African cultural retention, wrote:

> Probably never before in history has a people been so nearly completely stripped of its social heritage as the Negroes who were brought to America. Other conquered races have continued to worship their household gods within the intimate circle of their kinsmen. Through force of circumstances, they had to acquire a new language, adopt new habits of labor, and take over, however imperfectly, the folkways of the American environment. Their children's children have often recalled with skepticism the fragments of stories concerning Africa which have been preserved in their families. But, of the habits and customs as well as the hopes and fears that characterized the life of the forebears in Africa, nothing remains.[41]

Africans did not arrive on American soil as cultural and religious destitutes. They clung to their traditions and beliefs and often practiced them—although in secret—and adapted them in creative ways for whenever their captors tried to share Christianity with them or impose it upon them.[42]

Any gathering of Africans that represented some degree of physical and cultural independence likely created anxiety among whites. In spite of the suppression of their African beliefs and practices, slaves often exhibited an unquenchable craving for their own worship space. In Sea Island dialect is the report of one slave regarding the experience of a fellow slave named Okra, who wanted to maintain his African culture by building a hut that resembled the hut he built in Africa:

> Old man Okra he say want a place like he have in Africa so he build 'im a hut. I 'member it well. It was 'bout twelve by fo'teen feet an' it have dirt floor and he built the side like basket weave with clay paster on it. It have a flat roof what he make from bush and palmetto and it have one door and no windows. But massa make 'im pull it down. He say he ain't want no African hut on de place.[43]

The Africans' desire to retain their traditions evidently had a strong appeal particularly with the first generation of Africans in America. Even for the first hundred and fifty years of slavery in the New World, the masses of Africans were not attracted to American Christianity. Among the barriers to conversion, the following factors are noteworthy: (1) Many slaveholders appear to have had little interest in religion, much less in promoting it among their slaves—unless the kind of religion the slaves could be made to adopt would make them at once industrious and docile. (2) Many slaveholders apparently also resented the loss of productivity that would result if slaves spent too much time in religious activities. European methods of catechism and religious instruction were time consuming and labor intensive. (3) Recently imported slaves had difficulty understanding (to say nothing of adapting to) the language and culture of their captors. (4) And even after the linguistic and cultural barriers had been overcome, many African Americans characterized the religion of European Americans as dull, hypocritical, and unappealing.[44]

CONVERSION AS MUTUAL CHANGE: BLACK AND WHITE IN THE GREAT AWAKENING

Revivalism in Colonial America originated in European pietism, a negative response to the orthodoxy and rationalism of the seventeenth century. Across the Atlantic, particularly in Germany and Britain, there was a growing hunger for a more personal and less formal religion. Philip Jakob Spener (1635–1705) and August Hermann Francke (1663–1727) were prominent figures in fashioning the European pietism that ultimately spread to America.[45] Spener, the father of German pietism, published *Pia Desideria,* in which he stressed equal responsibility of the laity and clergy for ministry, or the priesthood of all believers. Pietism embraced by Spener focused on sanctification and holy living rather than on doctrine. Francke, a disciple of Spener, emphasized the practice of Christian living. A common thread in pietism was its embrace of an emotional response to accompany conversion. Of his own conversion, Francke said, "Sadness and anxiety immediately left my heart. And I was suddenly overcome by a wave of joy, such that I praised and magnified God aloud, who had granted me such grace."[46]

The spiritual fervor that accompanied the Great Awakening had affinities with the visible elements of African religion—elements that appeared less frequently in the more formal catechetical style of religious transformation—and elements of pietism. The shouting, dancing, and spirit possession embraced by European Americans in the era of the Great Awakening had significant appeal to Africans. The focus on music, on dance, on call and response, on hand clapping, on spirit possession, and on demonstrative worship was common then and now in many southern Baptist and Methodist churches. These Africanisms began to resonate and to unify the religious experiences and cultures of Africans and European Americans:

> [The styles of the Baptists and Methodists] were less formalized and stereotyped than that of the Presbyterian or Episcopal churches and the evangelical mode of preaching seemed to have a spontaneous appeal to the Negroes; perhaps, they were disposed toward emotionally toned group meetings by their African background. They seemed to have a marked selectivity for the intensity and emotionalism of the Baptist and Methodist preaching.[47]

Revivalism was the result of the spreading European pietism in the colonies, which gave birth to the particularly American forms

of demonstrative worship and spontaneous conversion characterized evangelical Christianity. The roots of the Great Awakening
also were grounded in the pietism of Wesley, who was a spiritual
heir of the Moravians. Wesley admitted that he was a nominal
Christian prior to his 1736 encounter with Moravians when he
was en route from Britain to Georgia to minister to Native
Americans of the tribe of Creek. Traveling by ship to fulfill his
mission in Georgia, Wesley passed through a life-threatening
storm and was visibly shaken with fear. On board the ship with
Wesley were Moravian missionaries who exhibited serenity and
calmness in the midst of the crisis. Wesley's encounter with the
Moravians exposed the weakness of his traditional faith and the
need for a more personal relationship with God. Wesley sought
the counsel of the Moravian Gottlieb Spangenberg about walking
closely and intimately with God. Spangenberg asked Wesley if he
knew Jesus Christ. Wesley replied, "I know He is the Savior of the
world." The answer was too evasive and not personal enough for
the Moravian, so he asked, "But do you know He has saved
you?" Wesley replied, "I hope He had died to save me." This still
was not satisfactory, so the Moravian asked, "Do you know your-
self?" Wesley said, "I do."[48] Prior to this experience, Wesley professed a faith he did not personally possess. This was true in spite
of the fact that he had been nurtured in a devout Christian home
where his father was an Anglican priest and his mother, Susanna
Welsey, was the proud daughter of a dissenting priest.

Pietism created the spiritual milieu that nurtured both Wesley
and George Whitefield. The same pietism inspired Jonathan
Edwards to seek proselytes in America with a personal and evangelical Christianity. This intercontinental pietism also inspired
Wesley and Whitefield's concerns about the spiritual well-being of
African slaves in America. Both evangelists ministered to slaves;
however, Welsey went beyond Whitefield in denouncing the institution of slavery itself.

Upon Wesley's initial evangelistic pilgrimage to America in
1732, he offered spiritual guidance to slaves in South Carolina.
Wesley was profoundly impressed with the spiritual fervor and
pietism expressed by the Africans who attended worship services.
According to Wesley's journal, he baptized his first African con-

verts into the Methodist movement in 1758. William B. McClain, in his book, *Black People in the Methodist Church*, called Wesley's first African converts "the unnamed two": "I preached at Wandsworth . . . in Mr. Gilbert's house. Two Negro servants of his and a Mulatto appear to be much awakened."[49]

Knowing of the large numbers of unevangelized Africans without a shepherd stirred the organizational adrenaline in Wesley, and he exhorted preachers to travel on foot and by horse from town to plantation to small farm, urging slaveholders to grant their slaves permission to attend public worship. Methodist preachers' dedication to the evangelism of slaves inspired the saying that on cold winter days "there is nothing out . . . but crows and Methodist preachers."[50]

The focus on personal and experimental religion, with status based on the new birth or conversion, tended to level all men and women before God as sinners in need of deliverance. The climate of intimacy and equality created by the conversion experience provided an environment for Blacks and Whites to share their different religious cultures. There was an inherently democratic and egalitarian proclivity in the spirited awakening that provided the abolitionists with the ammunition to condemn slavery as inconsistent with the teaching of the gospel.[51]

As African religion and culture were exposed to Western Christianity, there emerged a new religion that satisfied and accommodated both African and European understandings of religion. Many scholars agree that the Great Awakening of the eighteenth century included the conversion of large numbers of African Americans as well as Whites at revivals and camp meetings.[52] Africans and Europeans naturally differed in religious experience, but they shared significant aspects of the same faith. Both the Europeans and African slaves acknowledged an ultimate reality and another world that could not be seen, and revelation was the way people could know of this other world.[53] One woman who was sold into slavery and sent to Mississippi to work on a cotton plantation gave the following testimony after her conversion:

> I rejoice every day of my life for I know that I have another home—a house not made with human hands. A building is

waiting for me back in eternal glory and I have no need to fear. I came from Heaven and to Heaven I am now returning.[54]

Blacks and Whites found common ground at revivals during the Great Awakening. They shared a need for change. And death and sin theologically transcended race, class, creed, and national origin. As Robin Horton's insightful article on African conversions points out, "spiritual hunger" is the driving force of conversion, and it ushers in a wind of change.[55] Blacks and Whites who were converted were hungry for spiritual and physical renewal and transformation. Poor Whites felt excluded from the more established Anglican Church, which was perceived as elitist. Neither did Blacks feel welcome in the highly structured services of the Anglican Church. Therefore, the first awakening took place outside all established church structures and in the smaller and less structured Baptist and Methodist churches.

Many scholars who have taken an interest in the conversion experience have focused solely on slaves' desire for deliverance from physical bondage, which is an oversimplification of their desires. Black slaves, like Whites, had a strong desire to be delivered from their personal sins and shortcomings. The Reverend Samuel Davies, in 1757, recognized African Americans' spiritual confusion and existential need: "Many of them seem only to desire to be, they know not what. They feel themselves uneasy in their present condition and, therefore, desire a change."[56] Conversion for African Americans was a holistic change. It included physical and spiritual rebirth. "Being born again" was the conversion language best suited to the African-American religious experience. The new birth meant more than being liberated from slavery and physical bondage, as important as that was. Davies estimated that more than seven thousand African Americans attended his ministry at the different churches he established in Virginia[57] because they were looking for freedom from their spiritual and physical captivity. He was so impressed with black participation that he quoted the words of the psalmist to describe the phenomenon: "Ethiopia has stretched forth her hands unto God."[58]

In reading the original narratives of many slave conversion

experiences, one comes away with the impression that the new birth was marked by a sudden change of heart, with an abrupt change in the orientation of attitudes and beliefs. The new birth radically affected one's outlook on life and conception of the self. Thus the new birth best described the radical conversion experience of the African slaves.

In Albert Raboteau's *Slave Religion*, he tells the story of a slave named Praying Jacob, who was converted while attending a revival in Maryland. The crucial event empowered him to defy his master and ultimately to gain his utmost respect. The story goes that Praying Jacob became a devout believer and prayed three times a day, but his master, Saunders, was unsaved and forbade his slaves to practice religion on his plantation. Master Saunders warned Praying Jacob to refrain from praying, but Jacob insisted on praying three times a day. No matter what his work was or where he might have been, he would stop to pray. His master pointed his gun at him and told Praying Jacob that if he did not stop praying he would shoot him. After Praying Jacob finished his prayer, he told his master, "Your loss will be my gain—I have two masters, one on earth and one in heaven—master Jesus in Heaven and master Saunders on earth. I have a soul and body; the body belongs to master Saunders, and the soul to Jesus."[59] The lewd and lascivious Master Saunders would come to the field half drunk, raging like a madman and whipping the other slaves, but whenever he came to Jacob, Jacob would kneel down and pray and Master Saunders would not strike this man of God.[60] Praying Jacob believed that putting the fear of his master over the fear of God put his salvation in jeopardy. Similarly, C. Eric Lincoln and Lawrence H. Mamiya have observed that some slaves believed "unfreedom puts at risk the promise of salvation."[61] Consequently, the enslavement of the body did not necessarily mean the enslavement of the soul.

James Albert Ukawsaw Gronniosaw, a slave, recorded the original testimony of one slave's conversion experience as follows:

> One night I went to the mourner's bench—I seemed to have the weight of the house on me—and I was in darkness. And whilst I was down on my knees, I looked up and didn't see no house-top

or sky. I just saw clear heavens and it looked milkish and I said, "Lord, what is this?" And He said, "It is love." Then a shower of rain came down on the top of my head and went to the toes and I was just as light as any feather and I had on a white robe and I sailed and went upwards. Then, I met a band of angels, angels who were praising God and they looked at me and said, "Praise ye the Lord." The next morning I thought I didn't have any religion and I heard a voice saying, "I have chosen you out of the world. Go tell the people what I've done for you." And I went in the house and the voice came to me from the east singing: "Your sins are all washed away, free, free, my Lord. Your sins are all washed away, free, free, my Lord. Your Father done set you free."[62]

The "new birth" for this African slave was a "washing away of all [his] sins." In Gronniosaw's conversion narrative, the slave used the metaphor of a "shower of rain came down on the top of my head and went to the toes." In other words, this total person was changed and cleansed. The metaphor of water was very important in the conversion motif. It represented an agent for cleansing, for washing the sinner's sins away.[63]

Conversion to Christianity did not mean the same thing to all slaves. Likewise, their terms for conversion were varied, depending upon individual circumstances. For some, conversion meant a recrimination and a coming to terms with their disintegrated lives. For others, it was a way to express defiance toward their masters and the institution of slavery. Still others believed every word of the fire-and-brimstone preaching of white evangelists and sought forgiveness of their personal sins. One missionary observed that "those slaves who enjoyed the greatest freedom and had to face the fewest obstacles were also the least likely to become converts." [64] For slave women "'who no longer wished to allow themselves to be abused for sinful purposes,' conversion was a deterrence against the bestiality of the white masters."[65] Slaves and slaveholders employed conversionist language in a variety of situations in order to accomplish their respective goals.

The institution of slavery forced African Americans to accommodate two levels of religion. Slaves were put into a situation where they had to struggle to retain their African culture and at the same time adapt to European beliefs, culture, values, standards, and customs. Consequently, Blacks developed contradictory norms of conduct and values. On the one hand, they were called upon to be totally human, but on the other hand, they were expected to conduct themselves and to be treated as though they were subhuman and inherently inferior to white people. Similarly, the nature of salvation and the new birth called for freedom and responsibility, but enslavement required Blacks to be docile, childlike, and obedient. Africans had an arduous task of grappling with these conflicting values. As Africans learned the English language and became more and more acculturated to the American lifestyle, each successive generation became further alienated from its indigenous and ancestral values and practices.

Consistent growth in the number of Blacks being converted to Christianity did not occur until the latter half of the eighteenth century. That half century is therefore rightfully characterized by Peter H. Wood as the era of black preaching.[66] The period saw, for example, the emergence of such notable black preachers as David George, George Liele, Andrew Bryan, and Andrew Marshall. African Americans were more attracted to their own preachers than to white ministers. Black preachers likely had more credibility with slaves, who were attracted to Jesus as the great liberator of the body as well as the soul.

John Marrant's conversion by George Whitefield and other conversions by other great preachers were more the exception than the rule. The white religious establishment was in time disturbed that Blacks were being converted to Christ by their own African preachers. An Anglican minister in Brunswick, North Carolina, John Barnett, wrote disapprovingly in 1766: "The most illiterate among them are their Teachers [and] even Negroes speak in their meetings."[67] Prior to the Revolutionary War and in the decade following the war, many newspapers running ads asking for the capture of runaway slaves noted not only looks, clothing, age, height, and weight, but also religious dispositions. A notice in the 1777 *Virginia Gazette* sought the runaway William Hunt, a blacksmith and cobbler, and stated that "he pretends also to know something of religious matters, and misses no opportunity of holding forth on that subject." The next year, the same paper ran an ad for a runaway named Nat, observing that he "pretends to be very religious, and a *Baptist* teacher."[68]

43

The Anglican missionary work, revivalists, pious planters, evangelical white preachers, and teachers set the stage for the emergence of independent black preachers. With an increased leadership role, black preachers became catalysts for the conversion process. This established them as mediators between the slave community and the slave masters. The black preachers' role in the conversion process demanded literacy and leadership skills. Mastering the English language came to have a direct connection with soul winning. Early black preachers took advantage of their new status and contacts to attain literacy. David George, an early black preacher and one of the founders of the first independent black Baptist churches, solicited the help of his master's children to teach him to read. George celebrated his literacy with this testimony: "The reading so ran in my mind, that I think I learned in my sleep. . . . I can now read the Bible, so that what I have in my heart, I can see again in the scripture."[69] Learning to read served slave preachers well on two accounts: Literacy enhanced their effectiveness in saving souls and providing ministerial leadership to the slave community, and literacy helped to disarm the charge that Blacks were inherently inferior.

It has been argued that African religious elements are the strongest African elements in African-American culture. The early African settlers in America held tenaciously to traditional culture. Even after Africans began to speak English, Anglican missionaries continued to lament the African "attachment to the idolatrous Rites and Practices of their own Country."[70] However, with succeeding generations of Blacks being born in America, the systematic rite of separation attempted to divest African Americans of their culture, names, history, beliefs, and African past. This played a role in minimizing many African beliefs and practices.

The Africans who survived the horror of the middle passage became the primary participants in the institution of American slavery. America's peculiar institution was unknown to English law and in many respects unique in history. Because many of the American slaveholders professed Christianity, the need to justify slavery as a benevolent institution became as important to the slave masters as it had been to the slave traders. The Africans' need for conversion and civilization continued to captivate the minds of the slaveholders as the most humane rationale and defense of slavery. The conversion motif is what inspired the religious and civil authorities to provide religious training for slaves, which gave the slaves not only the possibility to become converts but also the opportunity to become literate. A discussion of slaves' literacy is in the next chapter.

CHAPTER TWO

Conversion and Religious Training: Religion with Letters [1700–1799]

Conversionist language was used by church and civil authorities to seek support and permission from slaveholders to evangelize their slaves. One of the strongest arguments in the conversionist language to justify slavery was that slavery exposed Blacks to Christianity and to the possibility of conversion. The evangelistic appeal was powerful, causing those slaveholders who may have doubted the ethics of human bondage to believe that if they owned slaves—with the intention of introducing them to Christianity—slaveholding would not be sinful but instead would be a benediction. Many religious and civil authorities endorsed religious training for slaves, which meant teaching slaves to read and write, often called "religion with letters." The conversion motif inspired the religious and civil authorities to provide religious training for slaves, which gave slaves not only the possibility to become converts but also the opportunity to become literate.

One thing many opponents and proponents of slavery had in common was a mutual interest in the religious training of slaves.

An early printed protest against slavery admonished slaveholders not only to set the captives free but also to "teach [Blacks] to read, and give them a Christian Education."[1] New Englander Cotton Mather was an advocate for the training of Blacks. In his essay "The Negro Christianized," Mather stressed the need for scholars who would teach Blacks to read and write.[2] Carter G. Woodson, the founder of Black History Week (now Black History Month) said, "The first real educators . . . [to enlighten] American Negroes were clergymen interested in the propagation of the gospel among the heathen of the new world."[3]

Even in the seventeenth century, there were advocates of slavery who also favored the education of Africans to prepare them to receive Christian instruction. For example, Philip II, the king of Spain, at first allowed only Christian slaves to be brought to America, hoping they might help evangelize the early Native Americans. Later, however, economic considerations changed Spanish evangelistic priorities.[4] With the opening of mines across the Americas (including the Caribbean, Peru, Mexico, and Granada) and the increased need for cheap labor, colonists urged the indiscriminate importation of slaves to meet labor demands. As the Spaniards' need for African labor intensified, they continued to instruct and train their slaves, because the Spanish felt that educated slaves would be more useful to Christian society.[5] French settlers in the New World also encouraged the education of their slaves. The French saw the education of slaves as an ethical demand: It was their duty to give slaves an education in exchange for their labor. Even as the growing demand for slave labor intensified, the French and Spanish Jesuits continued to advocate instruction for slaves.

While the French and Spanish encouraged the education of Blacks, the Spanish custom of miscegenation also facilitated the instruction of Africans. Many early settlers coming to America for commercial reasons left their families behind.[6] As a result, many of these early settlers cohabited with and married women of color, creating a mixed population. Unlike the English colonists, the Spanish, in particular, liberated their mulatto children and recognized them as equal.[7] As the Spanish and French competed with the English for the conquest of land and the conversion of souls, the success of Catholic missionaries aroused the interest of British Protestants, who became more vigilant in their own missionary efforts to Blacks.[8]

Despite opposition from the planters, the first school established in the colony of Virginia, in Accomac County, for Native Americans and Blacks was started by the Anglican Church.[9] Anglican missionaries called on the slaveholders in Virginia to educate and instruct their heathen slaves in the Christian faith. Much of the teaching focused on the young. Planters were encouraged to have all Native American, Negro, and mulatto children baptized and catechized by the time the children were fourteen years of age. Planters who taught their young slaves the Apostles' Creed, the Lord's Prayer, and the Ten Commandments were rewarded with a tax break until the slaves reached the age of eighteen. In short, civil and religious authorities collaborated in supporting the conversion and religious training of slaves.

The efforts to train and educate Blacks met with opposition from many planters who refused to cooperate. Opponents of religious instruction for Negroes argued that Negroes were inherently inferior, making efforts to educate them useless; furthermore, instruction took too much time away from their work. Slave owners also lamented that training made their slaves lazy and proud.[10] Besides, they argued, slaves who learned to read did not have the ability to understand or interpret what they read.

The education of slaves in other southern regions of colonial America began when the Reverend Samuel Thomas came to Charleston in 1702. He discovered that Negroes and Native Americans around Cooper River and Goose Creek, South Carolina, needed instruction.[11] The Society for the Propagation of the Gospel—organized in 1701 as the missionary arm of the Anglican Church, working ardently to supply qualified ministers to Anglican parishes in the English colonies—sent Thomas to evangelize and provide religious training to Blacks and Native Americans. The evangelistic efforts of Thomas did not go unnoticed. Particularly, Captain Nairne and the Reverend Robert Stevens of Goose Creek reported that "Mr. Thomas is instructing the negroes . . . and . . . they have books."[12] Stevens also reported that the slaves belonging to Governor Moore were provided Bibles and the Book of Common Prayer by the Governor.[13] Thus the Bible and religious literature were the first textbooks for Africans. The desire to know the Word of God inspired and motivated slaves to learn to read.

The Reverend Thomas had only five students at first, but the number quickly increased to thirty-two. Soon, Thomas succeeded in teaching twenty to read. This notable beginning permanently settled the controversy for the Society for the Propagation of the Gospel regarding Africans' ability to learn quickly.[14]

When Thomas unexpectedly died in 1706, the Society appointed Dr. Francis LeJau as his successor to address the educational needs of slaves. LeJau was a French Protestant, a Huguenot. He was a savvy diplomat and noted for his administrative acumen. These qualities were useful in his new position because many slaveholders were skeptical of religious training for their slaves, fearing that training would make their slaves proud and rebellious. To appease slaveholders suspicious of educating slaves, LeJau appealed to the slaveholders' self-interest, promising that religious training would make slaves more controllable and loyal to their masters, and thereby ensuring the slaveholders' approval and cooperation in the religious education of their slaves. He also presented slaveholders with a formal written statement reassuring them that conversion would not change a slave's status as property. This document was an extremely significant declaration because it came as a direct answer to the cynicism some masters had concerning the Christianization of slaves. By securing legal acknowledgment that baptism did not mean emancipation of the body, but only of the soul, the Society for the Propagation of the Gospel augmented its program of Christianization and education of Africans.[15]

In 1710, LeJau celebrated his success by sending a letter to the Society giving an account of a sensational Negro scholar, whom he labeled as "the best scholar of all the negroes in [his] parish." The celebrated slave had read a book depicting the judgments of God chastising people for their sins. The slave shared the story with his master: "There would be a dismal time and the moon would be turned into blood, and there would be . . . darkness."[16] Other slaves overheard the man telling the narrative to their master. The story quickly changed into an angel appearing to the slave and giving him a book that spoke to him about fire and judgment. Slaveholders were paranoid about any religious language that made reference to judgment and to divine retribution. This incident confirmed their paranoia about educating slaves and made them realize that those slaves were beginning to understand the Christian concepts of sin and judgment. Always the astute administrator, LeJau renounced the slave's prediction and assured slaveholders that slaves would be carefully examined before they were taught to read in the slave community.

The first duty of missionaries sent to evangelize slaves was to win the confidence of slaveholders. Their causing opposition or dissention would lead slaveholders to send the missionaries away from their plantations and give up their mission. The cooperation of slave masters was vital to missionary ventures of slave evangelism. Without the permission of slaveholders, slaves were prohibited from Sunday worship and religious training. Consequently, missionaries did all in their power to appease slaveholders and reassure them that religion would make slaves better and more dependable servants.

Between 1706 and 1707, the Society enacted a policy that required plantations desiring a minister to be willing and able to provide some financial support for the maintenance of a ministry to slaves. In addition to providing a religious teacher to slaves, the Society also furnished literature such as annual sermons, catechisms, Bibles, prayer books, hymn books, and primers such as the popular *Latin Grammar* by William Lilly and *The Christian Schoolmaster* by Dr. John Talbot.[17]

Africans continued to surprise their captors and advocates. Prior to his death, LeJau recognized that some slaves were better suited for book learning, while others had a better aptitude for craftsmanship and manual skill.[18] White missionaries were amazed at the Africans' innate ability to learn, their imagination, and their sensitive nature to human tragedy. Because slaves had limited exposure to literature and the printed word, except through the Bible, their opinions and beliefs were shaped through the interplay of the Bible and their innate creativity and imagination.[19]

The plantation economy of the early South Carolina elite encouraged and promoted the arts and crafts that talented Africans brought to America from the motherland. African masons and woodworkers occasionally were sent to England to train with fine craftsmen. Then when fine craftsmen themselves, these Africans returned to build exquisite colonial homes for the Carolina aristocracy.[20] It was African slaves who cut down trees, planted fields, and made possible the tobacco, sugar, rice, and cotton production that helped create the early wealth of America. Because of the Africans' role in fulfilling the labor shortage in colonial America, a British scholar argued that "America was saved by Africa."[21]

Africans not only demonstrated that they were gifted with their hands but also proved to be just as proficient in their cognitive ability. With amazing rapidity, African slaves adapted to a new culture, learned to speak, read, and write a new language, and endured the burdens of bondage. The lack of formal training did not prevent African slaves from becoming effective teachers and preachers. They taught and ministered to their own people, and in some cases, taught white children. Black preachers even occasionally served white congregations.[22]

However, there were obstacles. The Stono Rebellion in 1739, a slave uprising in South Carolina, stirred up much fear, anxiety, and anger among slaveholders. As a result of the violent revolt, sixty people, including Blacks and Whites, were killed. The revolt intensified the fear that education would make slaves rebellious and less controllable. The fear, though unjust, was perspicacious: Education may have increased the slaves' sense of worth and may have provided slaves access to a common language about the intrinsic worth and rights of humans to equitable treatment. Also, education may have increased the slave's indignation at mistreatment—and more alarming to the slaves was that the grounds of mistreatment were from Christian and legal tradition.

Anglican Commissary Alexander Garden was a strong advocate for training Blacks to be masters of their own schools and to teach their own people. To diminish the fear of slaveholders allowing the training of their adult slaves, Garden advocated training twelve- to sixteen-year-old male slaves in the principles of the Christian religion as contained in the Church Catechism, the Bible, and Book of Common Prayer. [23] The Society for the Propagation of the Gospel initiated, at the suggestion of Bishop Thomas Secker, a program of identifying bright young Blacks to teach their parents and the other people of their race. The bishop was also instrumental in sending three African natives to England where they were trained to do missionary work in their African homeland. In 1741, the Society purchased two Blacks, Harry and Andrew, who were trained to serve as schoolmasters to their own people.

The pedagogical method of having young African slaves teach and train their own people was under Garden's supervision. He erected the first school for Blacks in Charleston, South Carolina, in 1744, with Harry and Andrew serving as its first teachers. The school opened with sixty young scholars who were enthusiastic and possessed an insatiable craving for knowledge. The program designers hoped to graduate thirty to forty pupils who were "well instructed in religion and capable of reading their Bibles to carry home and diffuse the same knowledge to their fellow slaves."[24]

However, in 1739, after the Stono Rebellion, laws were enacted that made educating slaves illegal. But these laws did not diminish the efforts of the Anglican missionaries in ministering to the spiritual and intellectual needs of slaves. Despite the law abolishing Negro education in South Carolina, the school survived until 1764. Even after the school closed, individuals continued to be strong advocates of Negro education. A staunch supporter of teaching blacks was prominent South Carolinian Eliza Lucas, who married Justice Pinckney, also an advocate of the moral and literary training of Blacks. Lucas tutored a few black children. The level of support Whites gave black education fluctuated, but there was seldom a time when there was no assistance at all.[25] Garden's proposal to train adolescent slaves to teach was the first deliberate and intentional effort to develop meaningful and constructive leadership in the slave community.

The Anglican colonial establishment began to recognize the emergence of two distinct communities—one white and the other black. In Garden's appeal to the Society to approve his plan of teaching young slaves to train other Blacks, he called the slave community "a nation within a nation."[26] In a letter to historian Frederic A. Bancroft, who traveled extensively in the South interviewing Blacks and Whites to gather primary materials on race and politics, Garden expressed the uniqueness of the slave community: "As among us, religious instruction usually descends from parents to children, so among them it must at first ascend from children to parents, or from young to old."[27] The first designated African-American teachers were the children who read the Bible and other instruction tracts in the evening, especially on Sunday, to men and women, to parents and grandparents, to husbands and wives, and to brothers and sisters. Garden and the Society members believed that if their method of instructing the young slaves continued "for the space of 20 years, the knowledge of the Gospel [among] the slaves would not be much inferior . . . to [that of] the white [servant class]."[28]

In spite of the ardent and faithful efforts of the Society for the Propagation of the Gospel, Anglicans had only minimal success in evangelizing and Christianizing African slaves. It was not until the advent of the First Great Awakening (1720–1742), accompanied by soul-stirring preaching, that slaves were converted in large numbers. An example of the mass conversion of slaves is the population of slaves on Hugh and Jonathan Bryan's plantation in South Carolina, where George Whitefield had remarkable success ministering. After lamenting the physical conditions of slaves while visiting the Bryan Good Hope Plantation in 1740, Whitefield also expressed a deep concern for the souls of black people.[29] The Bryan family played a decisive role in nurturing African-American religious and educational development.[30] One of the earliest black Baptist churches and educational institutions developed as a result of the informal gatherings on Bryan's plantation where slaves came to hear revivalist preachers.[31]

The Bryan plantation was an incubator for the independent black church movement and the training ground for the early leaders of the African-American religious experience. The focus on "new birth" during the Great Awakening provided a common ground for Blacks and Whites, rich and poor, to be recognized as part of God's elect and to be received as saints in the Body of Christ. The outcome of the gospel proclaimed on the Bryan plantation was not the emancipation of slaves but an affirmation of their humanity and of the *Imago Dei,* or the image of God, in them. Even though the slaves on the Bryan plantation were denied racial equality, the compassionate slaveholders acknowledged camaraderie of the soul that bound slaves and masters.

The Bryans were relentless advocates of educating slaves. Their training and spiritual virtue paved the way for the formation of the earliest black independent congregation in Savannah, which was under the ministerial leadership of Andrew Bryan, a slave of Jonathan Bryan. Andrew Bryan was converted under the influence and tutelage of George Liele, who was one of the earliest pioneer Negro preachers and a founder of the Baptist church in Silver Bluff, South Carolina.[32] Andrew Bryan was born a slave at Goose Creek, South Carolina, and continued the work George Liele had started along coastal South Carolina and Georgia. Under the apprenticeship of Liele, Andrew was an exhorter at prayer meetings held at the Bryan plantation home, Brampton. The Bryan family was one of the largest slaveholding families in the colonies, and the family provided unfailing support and opportunities for Bryan and Liele to preach and minister to slaves.

Eight or nine months after Andrew's conversion, he began preaching to Blacks and to a few Whites that gathered around him to hear God's Word. He was such a charismatic speaker that he successfully led his followers to erecting a simple building of worship at Yamacraw, on the outskirts of Savannah, Georgia. Andrew Bryan's success did not meet with the approval of some local Whites, and his work was impeded when he was beaten and arrested for causing insurrection among the slaves.[33] Bryan interpreted the setback and persecution as a badge of honor when he declared that he would "freely suffer death for the cause of Jesus Christ."[34]

The conversionist religion and redemptive suffering of Andrew Bryan won the favor of Chief Justice Henry Osborne, James Habersham, George Walton, and James Montague—all prominent white citizens of Savannah, Georgia, who supported and admired the tenacity of Bryan as he struggled to organize an independent black congregation. After Jonathan Bryan's death in 1788, Andrew Bryan's ministry was challenged by a Savannah grand jury. Abraham Marshall was the slave master in Savannah who licensed Bryan to preach. As an influential member of the Georgia Baptist Association, Marshall was summoned to examine the charges brought against Bryan and his disciples. Marshall exonerated Andrew and his followers, saying that they had "been brought out of darkness into the light of the gospel, believing it is the will of Jesus Christ to keep up His worship and ordinances."[35] Jonathan Bryan's son, William, continued the family legacy of supporting the ministry and training their slaves. William allowed Andrew to use the barn for worship until the estate was divided among the family. Andrew bought his freedom and a lot at Yamacraw, where he built his home and worshiped in a residence built for his brother, Sampson. Andrew's congregation grew rapidly. He had 225 full members and 350 converts, many of whom had not been given permission by their owners to be baptized.[36] To nurture his members and to provide religious education for them, the black pastor solicited copies of the Bible, catechisms, and John Bunyan's *Pilgrim's Progress* from his white friends.[37] The Reverend Joseph Cook, a white minister, wrote the following assessment of Andrew Bryan and his venture to build an independent black congregation:

> They began to rise from obscurity and appear great. [The pastor's] gifts are small but he is clear in doctrines of the gospel. I believe him to be truly pious and he has been the instrument of doing more good among the poor slaves than all the learned doctors in America. Meaning slaves responded better to black preachers than learned white preachers.[38]

The First Great Awakening laid the foundation and provided opportunities for the religious and intellectual development of Africans. Among the more than five hundred members of Andrew Bryan's congregation, fifty learned to read and three learned penmanship; however, many more African slaves had an insatiable desire to read and write. The Great Awakening relied on oral and written traditions to convey its messages, and proponents of evangelistic Christianity published extensively. For example, in preparation for George Whitefield's evangelistic crusade, hundreds of his printed sermons were circulated in the American colonies two years before his arrival. When Whitefield finally arrived, the colonial press printed thirty-three of his sermons. Eleven colonial newspapers from Boston to Charleston gave extensive coverage of his crusades, serving as advance publicity to mass outdoor services.[39]

The Great Awakening promoted literacy among both slave and free but played a considerable role in providing education to Africans. They saw the Great Awakening and Christianity as the only opportunity for literacy and learning all they could. The hunger slaves had for literacy inspired Whites to provide resources that would expand black educational opportunities. For example, William Bolton, former proprietor of a Philadelphia dancing room, experienced the new birth and converted his assembly hall into a "school for teaching children to read." The response was overwhelming. In twenty-three days, at least fifty-three black scholars enrolled in the school.[40]

With equal enthusiasm, slaves in Virginia responded to opportunities of learning to read. Samuel Davies, a Presbyterian evangelist, championed the cause of the instruction of slaves into the Christian faith. Davies encouraged slaveholders to support the efforts of providing religious training for slaves. He expressed his strong confidence in slaves' capacity to learn: "Your Negroes may be ignorant and stupid as to divine things," Davies wrote, "not for Want of Capacity, but for Want of Instruction." From his personal experience in teaching slaves to read, Davies declared, "I have Reason to conclude, that making Allowance for their low and barbarous Education, their imperfect Acquaintance with our Language, their having no Opportunity for intellectual Improvements, and the like, they are generally as capable of Instruction, as the white People."[41]

The drive Blacks exhibited for education helped them combat the Europeans' notion that they were inherently inferior, thus giving a significant blow to one of the major proslavery arguments. After Davies told of the passion his African converts had for learning, he began working with other missionaries to secure Bibles, hymnals, and spelling books for training slave converts. The conversion process and slaves' zeal for learning won the respect and admiration of Davies and many other white religious leaders. Davies wrote, with a great sense of pride, "The sacred hours of the Sabbath, that used to be spent in frolicking, dancing, and other profane courses, are now employed in attending upon public ordinances, in learning to read at home, or in praying together, and finding the praises of God and the Lamb."[42]

Slaves used religious conversion not only as a means to enter into a new spiritual world but also as an opportunity to become literate. They realized that learning to read the Bible would invigorate their self-respect. Those who were fortunate enough to secure a Bible cherished it, and some carried it with them everywhere. "The book will make me wise," one African said of the Bible.[43] On a few documented occasions, the Bible was used as a magic talisman to protect slaves from the masters' abuse. One incident of abuse involved a slave who was being assaulted by an overseer. She "took her Bible in hand and started to read him several passages from the text. The episode caused him to relent."[44] Priests and other educated, religious people were held in high esteem by slaves because slaves believed that literacy provided unique access to the supernatural. Slaves were insightful enough to realize that if God is revealed through the Bible, it was imperative to be able to read God's Word.[45]

A story is told about James Gronniosaw, who assumed that reading was magic. He first witnessed his captain reading on the slave ship sailing from Africa to America: "I was never so surprised in my whole life as when I saw the book talk to my master." Seeing the captain's lips move and hearing audible sounds, Gronniosaw assumed the book was talking to the captain. Gronniosaw then sought access to such powers: "When nobody saw me, I opened it and put my ear close upon it, in hope that it would say something to me."[46]

Laws prohibited Georgia, the buffer colony between South Carolina and Florida, from owning slaves until October 26, 1749. Consequently, the slave population did not grow rapidly. James Habersham, one of the founders of Georgia, reported that the town of Savannah had no more than twenty-five Blacks.[47] However, three months after slavery was legalized in Georgia, the Society for the Propagation of the Gospel was promoting religious training for Blacks by allotting resources for literature and a teacher to train slaves. Joseph Ottolenghe, a native of Casale,

Piedmont, Italy, was appointed catechist by the Society to train slaves. He was the son of a wealthy Jewish family in the silk business. After he was converted from Judaism to Christianity, he joined the Church of England and became a missionary to the Negroes and Native Americans in Georgia. Ottolenghe became an influential member of the Georgia colony's House of Representatives in 1755. He later became a tax collector and property assessor of the town and district of Savannah. As a result of his government service, he was granted large tracts of land that further expanded his opportunities to serve and educate slaves. In 1753, he built a large house that served as his home and as one of the first schools for slaves in Georgia.[48]

The First Great Awakening made learning necessary and more accessible to Africans. The opportunities and methods by which they learned, however, varied from place to place. James Gronniosaw was the slave of New York evangelist Theodore Frelinghuysen. Frelinghuysen sent Gronniosaw to school, and Frelinghuysen's wife supplied him books.[49] A Virginia slave known as Uncle Jack paid his master's children to teach him to read, giving them fruit and nuts in exchange for instruction.[50]

As African Americans learned, they began their own theology and interpretation of scriptures that was compatible with their own experiences and temperaments. A visitor to a slave plantation's religious service observed that after the white pastor delivered the dull homily, a slave exhorter was allotted a few minutes to respond by providing the practical application of the sermon delivered by the white preacher. The visitor was more impressed with the slave's response to the sermon than with the sermon and concluded that the black preacher's response "was showing the white brother how he should have preached." The observer critiqued the white minister's attempt at preaching as dry and powerless. No one can move the Negro but a Negro, he observed; the Negro alone understands the avenue to blacks' emotions and sympathies.[51] African slaves brought spirit and vitality to American Christianity; they sustained remnants of the fervor and enthusiasm generated by the revivals of the Great Awakening. Slaves had a genius for phrase making and dramatic situations.[52] A visitor to a Sunday afternoon evangelical African worship service noted the "peculiar element of Negro worship," which was devotional singing: "[The Negro's] singing is not artistic . . . but you can hardly keep from weeping under its influence."[53]

Others were not as impressed with the peculiar style of worship of African slaves as the aforementioned observer. Francis LeJau cautioned slaveholders that their "best [Negro] scholar . . . through his learning was [likely] to create . . . confusion" among his fellow slaves for putting "his own constructions upon his reading of the holy prophets."[54] What LeJau labeled confusion was in reality competition because black preachers' interpretation of religion was more palatable to slaves than the religion of their oppressors. The religion the white preacher offered Blacks was generally intended to make them docile, obedient servants to their masters. In contrast to white preachers, slave exhorters were more likely to focus on freedom and liberation, which slave owners and LeJau discouraged. Disappointed with the outcome of religious training that was producing independent and assertive Blacks, LeJau denounced African slaves "for lacking judgment enough to make good use of the learning."[55]

Nevertheless, the first public mixed assembly of Blacks and Whites was in church. The uniqueness of Southern religion, even today, is that there has been a cross-fertilization and fusion of religious experiences and practices between Blacks and Whites. Charles Woodman, an Anglican minister, was amazed by the degree of racial mixture in churches of the Carolina backcountry during the 1760s. He described one congregation as "a body of people assembled—such a medley, such a mixed multitude of all colors and complexion I never saw."[56] It was not unusual during the colonial period, especially during the Great Awakening, for Blacks and Whites to worship together. Granted, white congregations set certain limitations about slaves' preaching and participation in the governance of the church, but the church provided the first public place for the two races to assemble for worship and religious training. Evangelical Christianity, embraced by the Great Awakening, enhanced the opportunity for black leadership in the slave community and occasionally in white congregations.[57]

Slave preachers' delivery was usually rhythmic and witty. A few slave preachers were licensed after serving an apprenticeship under a white overseer, but most were unlicensed charismatic exhorters. They were able to survive the horror of human bondage and then manipulate the system in a manner that enabled them to create a sense of unity and solidarity in the slave community.[58] A few of the early pioneering black preachers were: Josiah (or Jacob) Bishop, who effectively pastored a mixed congregation in Portsmouth, Virginia. In 1792, his church gave him money to purchase his freedom. William Lemon served as pastor of a white Baptist church in Gloucester County, Virginia, in the late 1790s. "Old Captain" organized Blacks in Lexington, Kentucky, even though he was denied a name for himself and for his organization. Joseph Willis was one of the pioneering black Baptist pastors in Bayou Chicot, Louisiana. He was elected the first president of Louisiana's Baptist Association.

The slave preacher was both a prophet and a priest. He (and occasionally, she) was a seer (prophet) that spoke for God and occasionally performed priestly functions such as officiating at weddings and baptizing new converts. The slave preacher was the first and foremost leader of the African community. The popularity and influence wielded by the slave preacher sometimes threatened the master's control; therefore, the preacher was always watched with suspicion. Some slaveholders had a distrust of preachers, and if preachers alluded to freedom in any way, their privileges of preaching and sometimes living were jeopardized.

Some slaves cultivated an intimacy with their masters that enabled them to invite their masters and their families to revivals they were preaching, and upon occasion, some masters were converted. When this happened, the slave preacher became an instant celebrity on the plantation among Blacks and Whites. Eminent plantation slave preachers were larger-than-life celebrities.

But the inability to read did not negate a slave's ability to preach. The imagination, originality, and informality that characterized black preaching complemented the spirit of the Great Awakening. The slave preacher was depicted as "the most unique personality developed by the Negro on American soil."[59] The slaves respected those who could understand and interpret the circumstances they had to endure. A call to preach from God was also a call to prestige, power, and the deepest service within the slave community.[60]

America is deeply indebted to slave religion for the unique preaching style of the black preacher and the unique contribution African Americans still make to the cultural and religious experience of America. For example, the antiphonal African call and response gives rhythm to the sermon. And it was these unique sermons that provided slaves on the brink of despair with a citadel of hope.[61] So slave preachers were not only leaders and educators in the slave community, but also the first counselors and social workers among their people. But it is impossible to understand the full impact black preachers had on saving African-American people from despair and disaster. In pursuit of their calling, black preachers were without academic degrees but never without the dignity of their office. They were without honor, but not without integrity. The slave preachers were denied visible church buildings but not the invisible Spirit. They were often stymied but never completely stifled. Slave preachers were the spokespersons for their people with the longest tenure of leadership, dating back to the moment black people were brought to America as slaves.[62]

However, the education received by some black ministers actually distanced them from their members. Some educated preachers came to disdain elements of African religion and culture in worship, even denouncing some of the indigenous beliefs and practices of their own people. For example, in 1873, Jonathan Gibbs, a Dartmouth-educated Presbyterian black minister, lamented the ecstatic religious behavior of black people who "still preach and pray, sing and shout all night long."[63] Some African-American ministers trained in northern universities were viewed as "mis-educated," trained as black preachers in seminary to be white men and women in black skin.[64]

From colonial times to the present, some Blacks have appreciated the cross-fertilization of American Christianity and the African religious experience, while others have viewed African religion through the eyes of white oppressors. For example, Jupiter Hammon expressed his gratitude for American Christianity in a poem to Phillis Wheatley. He wrote, "Thou hast left the heathen shore,/ Thro' mercy of the Lord,/ Among the heathen live no more,/ Come magnify thy Lord."[65] Wheatley compared the light of the new birth with the darkness of paganism. The poet declared:

> Let us rejoice in and adore the wonders of God's infinite love in bringing us from a land semblant of darkness itself, and where the divine light of revelation (being obscured) is in darkness. Here the knowledge of the true God and eternal life are made manifest; but there was nothing in us to recommend us to God. . . .[66]

The conversion process was the most civil vehicle to bring about intimacy and relationship between the slaves and the slaveholders. Religious training provided slaves with the rudiments for learning to read and write. The first schools for Blacks were not only sponsored by religious institutions but also often in one room in rural church buildings.

Conversion, which was often used to preserve the institution of slavery, actually commenced the intimate relationship between education and religion in the African experience. Through the Christianization and education programs of the Society for the Propagation of the Gospel, disinherited African slaves inadvertently received the linguistic rudiments for a more personal and meaningful religious experience during the Great Awakening. In short, the conversion motif created the impetus for the whole enterprise of African-American education, which, in turn, made it possible for Blacks in America "to become readers and, [after] passing out of slavery, to have their own churches, bishops, colleges, and institutions."[67]

CHAPTER THREE

Conversion and the Plantation Missions: Religion Without Letters [1800–1865]

After the Revolutionary War, the Second Great Awakening (1780–1830) helped the new nation take shape and communicate its goals and values. With its social reform and humanitarian initiatives, revivalist Christianity empowered and stimulated antislavery sentiments. Revivalism contributed to the ongoing debates of certain formative themes and issues that helped shape the ideologies of the United States. One of the most debated issues was slavery. The South continued to defend slavery as a necessary, benevolent institution, but the North was in favor of abolishing slavery.

By the end of the eighteenth and the beginning of the nineteenth centuries, evangelical Christianity had experienced unprecedented growth among African Americans. The denominations that benefited the most from this pietistic Christianity were Baptist and Methodist denominations. Slaves living in or near towns and cities had the opportunity to attend church with their masters.

There were even a few instances of emerging independent black churches. For example, the Gillfield Church of Petersburg, Virginia, was an early independent Baptist church. Another black Baptist church, discussed in the previous chapter, was formed in Silver Bluff, South Carolina. George Liele, who was involved in the formation of the Silver Bluff Baptist Church, was also one of the founders of the first African Baptist Church of Savannah, Georgia, in 1779. In the early 1800s, two other African Baptist churches were established in Savannah, Georgia. But the vast majority of Blacks lived on plantations, away from these urban black churches and well beyond their influence. However, all major church bodies in the South began to address the sensitive issue of slavery and to evangelize to, and Christianize, slaves as black membership and participation in the churches increased. As a result of the North and South's opposing views on such a large issue, all mainline denominations split by the mid–nineteenth century. An example of the split took place in 1844 when the Methodist Episcopal Church became the Methodist Episcopal Church South and the Methodist Episcopal Church, the northern contingent.

After the divisions, it became even more important for southern denominations to have a vigilant and aggressive mission of converting slaves. The incentive for Southerners to evangelize their slaves was combating the growing abolitionist fervor in the North and the charge that the South was neglecting the spiritual welfare of its slaves. The Northern abolitionist movement caused the South to become even more suspicious of the infiltration of plantations with antislavery teachings and literature.

Then there were two plots that shocked South Carolina. The first was the Camden Insurrection of 1816, which resulted in the passage of the Acts of 1818 that increased overseers' patrol of the plantation mission services and limited manumission.[1] The Denmark Vesey Plot of 1822 also served as a rude awakening of the inherent restlessness and desire for freedom in the slave community. These incidents intensified the white community's skepticism of religion for slaves because evidence pointed to the free Negro church in Charleston as having masterminded the plots. The investigation showed that Vesey, the instigator, and Gullah

Jack, Mundy Gell, Peter Poyas, and several other conspirators were members of the African Church, which was consequently dissolved.[2] During the aftermath of these incidents, planters were obsessed with the fear of future slave revolts. Because of the reaction of southern Whites to slave conspiracies and abolitionist agitation, some African Baptist churches were required to assimilate with white churches. This was the case with Elam Baptist Church in Charles City, Virginia, where slaves were transferred by their owners to a church under white control. However, a more drastic measure was taken with the African Baptist Church at Williamsburg, Virginia; it was closed.[3]

In the aftermath of the slave revolts of the 1800s, slaves' religious education changed, partly in reaction to David Walker's *Appeal* in 1829, in which Walker argued for massive slave insurrections, and partly in reaction to increasing abolitionist propaganda.[4] Walker's revolutionary *Appeal* generated an insecure climate and fear among white Southerners. They responded to the *Appeal* by passing laws to suppress the seditious tract and to prevent the circulation of other such inflammatory literature. A group of Georgia men offered a reward of $1000 for Walker dead and $10,000 for Walker alive. And they vowed to fast from eating until Walker was captured.[5]

In response to slave insurrections of the nineteenth century and increased propaganda from Walker and others, civil authorities enacted laws that forbade the meetings of Blacks unless a white person was present and that prohibited the literacy of slaves. Civil authorities held the religious community responsible for implementing religious instruction that would not infringe upon civil statutes. In response to the authorities' new law, churches altered slaves' religious training.

Many denominations united in their efforts of taking responsibility for the sanctioned religious training of Blacks. To meet the challenge, southern Protestant churches devised an oral method of religious training for African converts. Southerners, hoping to combat abolitionist propaganda and subsequent insurrections, approved the plan for the oral religious training for slaves, training which one scholar termed "religion without letters."[6]

Religion without letters denied slaves access to all religious literature, including the Bible. The question of why they received only oral instruction inevitably crossed their minds. The texts and scripture passages read to them were judiciously chosen in the conversionist language to fit the scheme of human bondage. Lunsford Lane, a North Carolina slave, who purchased his freedom and became an abolitionist, said he heard the text, "Servants, be obedient to your masters," and committed it to memory.[7] William Wells Brown, a fugitive abolitionist from Lexington, Kentucky, realized that slaveholders were much less concerned about saving their souls than about employing religion to make them good slaves. Brown wrote this assessment of the religious instruction to slaves:

> Their religious teaching consists in teaching the slave that he must never strike a white man, that God made him for a slave, and that when whipped, he must find fault . . . for the Bible says, "He that knoweth his master's will and doeth it not, shall be beaten with many stripes," and slaveholders find such religion very profitable.[8]

THE PLANTATION MISSIONS AND ORAL RELIGIOUS TRAINING

Prior to 1810, there was a virtual national consensus that the institution of slavery was a necessary evil designed to civilize Africans, who were considered culturally barbaric. There was an underlying assumption that through acculturation and assimilation, Blacks one day would have some semblance of cultural parity with Whites. The religious instruction that now demanded an oral education was important in the implementation of this process of assimilation.

However, the increased demand for labor and for free labor caused southern Whites to reappraise the institution of slavery and its future. Some white Southerners altered their attitude toward slavery for economic profitability, no longer calling it a temporary tutelage but a permanent benevolent institution in society. In addition, Southerners viewed Blacks as not only culturally inferior but also created and ordained by God to be "servants." Interpretations of Genesis 9:25 attempt to justify the enslavement of African peoples.

The conversion motif of the Second Great Awakening embraced more humanitarian impulses, which focused on changing the moral character of all society. Revivalists had a vision of being called by God as instruments to purify the earth in preparation for God's final act of redemption. Therefore, the conversion motif embraced the total life in society, and no phase of American life was left untouched. Temperance, Sabbath observance, world peace, profanity, vice, women's rights, slavery, correctional institutions, educational innovation—all eventually became issues of concern.

In addition to showing concern for slaves, conversionist language also enhanced the roles and importance of white women in the church and in society. Donald G. Mathews exemplifies a conversionist ritual that often preceded church membership. A converted woman would stand before the congregation and publicly profess her faith by giving an account of her conversion experience. Mathews says that the public acknowledgment of women's faith contributed to their sense of self-confidence.[9]

In many congregations, white women, like children, were expected to be seen but not heard. The spiritual revival represented a societal renaissance that expanded the roles and importance of women in the church. According to Winthrop S. Hudson, and John Corrigan, "Women may or may not have been more religious than men, but for women a conversion experience would provide some release from the constraints of male domination."[10] The new birth motif for white women as well as for slaves meant a new beginning in areas of life, including opportunities in the areas of church, home, and community leadership. During this transitioning time, the term "new birth" implied both spiritual and secular liberation. In short, the conversion process put women and Blacks at the center of attention before a congregation.[11] The conversion motif allowed them the freedom to speak before a congregation and be to honored and respected for their unique spiritual gifts. The revivalist, abolitionist, and temperance reformer, Theodore Dwight Weld, in a letter to Lewis Tappan written in 1835, typifies the conversionist language that embraced the diversity of spiritual gifts:

> God has called *some* prophets, *some apostles,* and some *teachers.* All the members of the body of Christ have not the same office. Let Delavan drive Temperance, McDowell moral Reform; Finney Revivals, Tappan antislavery, etc. Each of these is bound to make his own *peculiar* department his *main* business, and to promote *collaterally* as much as he can the other objects. I have no doubt but Finney has erred in not giving as much *collateral* attention to anti slavery as the present emergent crisis demands. And I am equally certain that I have not done as much collaterally to promote temperance and Revivals while I have been lecturing on slavery as I ought.[12]

One of the most inflammatory and divisive issues of the Second Great Awakening was the institution of slavery. The growing democratic belief was that all people should be free. The Awakening also tapped into the deeply rooted Puritan ethos that called for the transformation of the world. These guiding principles spawned the idea of abolishing slavery without granting slaves social, political, or economic equality. Northern evangelists viewed the South as a mission field where both slaves and slaveholders were in need of Christ's atoning grace to set them free. The most devastating charge abolitionists levied against the South was that the whole institution of slavery was a sin.

Southern church and civil authorities employed their best minds to defend the institution of slavery. The leading polemicists were southern educators and churchmen, including William A. Smith, Alexander McCaine, Patrick H. Mell, James Henley Thornwell, Richard Fuller, and others. But southern apologists continued to defend human bondage on the grounds that slavery was a benevolent institution created for the purpose of caring for a people who were innately incapable of providing for their own well-being.

CHURCH-SPONSORED PLANTATION MISSIONS

There was a concerted effort by all major southern denominations to provide religious instruction for the slaves in order to protect them from abolitionist propaganda. To this end, plantation missions became the missionary arm for delivering the appropriate conversionist language to slaves. Charles C. Jones, a Presbyterian and one of the masterminds of the plantation missions, cited the Liberty County Association in Georgia as a model for the implementation of the conversion process for slaves. In its third annual report, the Association used the following conversionist language regarding evangelism:

> We should protect ourselves by law, as far as possible, from the circulation of incendiary publications, and from the teachings of incendiary agents; and then should we look at home and enter upon a discharge of our duty to the Negroes, as will meet the approbation of God and our consciences, and commend ourselves to the consciences of other men. One important step toward discharge of our duty in a most effectual manner, we believe to be a general and judicious system of religious instructions.[13]

The conversion motif in the Association's report was the "judicious system of religion." The report inferred a method of instruction that would meet the approval of the southern establishment, modify the conscience of the slave community, and invoke God's blessing and understanding for slavery.

Church leaders sold the concept of plantation missions to slave owners by promising religious teaching and subsequent conversions that would make slaves more honest and reliable and also would protect the institution of slavery from innuendo propagated by abolitionists. Proponents of the mission initiatives maintained that "Christianity would regularize and pacify relations between slaves and masters."[14] The success of religious instruction to Negroes is reflected in the report of R. F. W. Alston of the Georgetown District in South Carolina, a cluster of Methodist churches supervised by a presiding elder:

> Those who have grown up under religious training are more intellectual and generally, though not always, more improved than

those who have instruction . . . as adults. Indeed the degree of intelligence which, as a class, they are acquiring is worthy of deep consideration.[15]

Slaveholders were encouraged to take plantation missions seriously because slaveholders already had a vested interest in their slave property, which provided them free labor. In 1829, Charles Cotesworth Pinckney Jr. addressed the Agricultural Society of South Carolina with an example of the planters' interest in missions. Pinckney said that these missions would cultivate "domestic happiness" and that the slaves would be "more anxious to promote their owners' welfare."[16] He maintained that assuming conversion and instruction of slaves would lead to more insurrections was erroneous. He did much to rouse slave masters to the benefits of conversion and to dispel the fears that had paralyzed religious activities in the region.[17]

The mission was designed to defend the institution of slavery and to disarm the abolitionist charge that southern Whites neglected the spiritual welfare of their slaves. The plantation mission was to be incorporated as integral to the members of the domestic plantation system, which included the slave master's family, overseer, and the slave quarters. The Protestant denominations assigned white ministers to supervise the missions and to preach in a conversionist language that would appease slaveholders and at the same time be adaptable to the background of slaves. Slaveholders responded to the appeal to support these missions in varying ways. The more receptive planters provided "praise houses" for slaves to worship under the supervision of a white pastor. Other planters refused to provide any religious instruction whatsoever for their slaves.

The "judicious system of religion" also called for denominations to assign their most talented preachers to ministering to blacks. "[As to] what kind of preachers are needed for the Negroes," Charles C. Jones said, "certainly not *ignorant* preachers." Jones further argued, "To put men to this work who are not only *unlearned* but *ignorant,* is to put the blind to lead the blind; and as a result, 'both shall fall into the ditch.'"[18] Church leaders recognized, although it was not judicious for them to admit it openly, the cognitive ability of Blacks. Leaders cautioned their denominations of adopting the attitude that any pastor or sermon would do for Negroes because "Negroes have been *wise* enough . . . and *proud* enough not [to put up] with any sort of a sermon and have therefore stayed at home."[19]

The examination and selection of men sent to preach to Negroes was crucial. They had to be men who would equivocate on the issue of slavery and had regional ties to, and empathy for, the South. It was imperative for preachers to be truly indoctrinated into the designed system of promoting slavery before attempting to minister to Blacks. Planters were paranoid over anything that encouraged the hope of freedom. Because it was a volatile time, preachers were cautioned to refrain from attacking the institution of slavery in a way that would bring down the wrath of the white community upon them and perhaps result in "dismissal from [their] chosen work."[20] To plant ideas of freedom or insurrection would bring condemnation upon the community and its ministry. Ministers were encouraged to communicate with slaveholders and slaves as long as communication did not change the sociopolitical climate.

The ministers' responsibility to their flock did not end on the Sabbath. They were charged with lecturing to the slaves at least once a week, visiting the sick, attending funerals, maintaining strict discipline, appointing watchmen as assistants, and appointing a committee of instruction from among white members to aid all persons applying for admission.[21] Plantation mission churches were composed of households that included parents, children, masters, and slaves; and it was the ministers' duty to watch over everyone in the church. In short, the minister was employed to monitor and sanction racial etiquette.

Ministers as well as lay members, deacons, and elders were encouraged to teach in the Sabbath schools. Sabbath schools were established to instruct children, youth, and adults. As teaching was done orally, children and youth benefited the most: "They will learn to use their memories and their reasoning powers and be prepared to profit by the more elevated services of the sanctuary."[22] The oral method required that the teacher first pose questions, state the answers, and then ask the class to repeat the questions and answers until both were memorized. The pedagogical formula, as one missionary put it, went like this: "We have no schools, teachers, nor scholars; for in this state there is a law prohibiting the teaching of letters to the slaves, [and] selling or giving them books of any description whatever; therefore we can only tender to them oral instruction. This is done by catechising the little Negroes, etc."[23] Through the Sabbath school, ministers formed a more intimate acquaintance with their Negro congregants. White ministers won the confidence and respect of slaves on the plantation, and the close relationship between ministers and slaves further ensured that the slaves would not be influenced by outside provocation.

Religious instruction also meant that ministers would convene meetings on the plantation with the knowledge and approval of the owner or manager of the estate.[24] One missionary reported:

> I have put a stop to all preaching by our black brethren when I found them engaging in activities contrary to the law of the state and the police of the country, and have encouraged them to hold prayer meetings twice a week, their leaders being present to direct the same, and to attend to their class meetings, according to the discipline, obtaining the owners sanction of the measure, which is readily granted.[25]

Even before the advent of plantation missions, slaves would gather secretly in remote swamps and thickets and worship away from the big house and the prying eyes of the overseer. These obscure places of worship, hidden from the eyesight of the slave master, were known as "invisible institutions." It was in these bush harbors that slaves vented their pent-up feelings of pain, sorrow, and supernatural joy in a spirit-filled manner. But the emergence of plantation missions did not replace the "invisible institutions" of fiery preaching, fervent prayers, and soulful singing; visible and invisible institutions existed simultaneously.

The two denominations most effective at delivering judicious religion to Negroes on the plantations were the Methodist and the Baptist denominations. This was due in part to a less formal and a more personal conversion they offered slaves. Methodists and Baptists were also successful because many of their ministers stayed on the plantations, along with the overseers. Residing on the plantation and providing permanent instruction to the Negroes were very important factors. Jones maintained these features would counter the abolitionist propaganda that Southerners neglected the spiritual welfare of Negroes and slave holders.[26]

While impediments to mission work among Blacks were many, one of the main obstacles was that Africans were only two or three generations removed from their native land and resisted giving up their ancestral culture and beliefs. They struggled to retain their African names, speech, and customs, which were mysteries to their masters. A missionary assigned to Blacks in the area of St. Helena, South Carolina, lamented, "There is great difficulty in conveying religious knowledge to the minds of adult Negroes who have grown up in ignorance."[27] This was a typical European-American assessment of the older generation of Africans that was reluctant to relinquish ancestral African names, culture, history, and beliefs. Since European Americans had little knowledge and appreciation of Africa's culture and its people, they suppressed, denounced, and ignored most African customs and beliefs as "ignorance." The same missionary who complained about his difficulty with adult Negroes reported with glee, "The children and youth receive and understand the instructions of their teachers with comparatively great readiness and ease and their intelligence and docility are decidedly improved."[28] In fact, those who ministered to the slave community pointed out that the most positive outcomes of education came from children and youth. It never occurred to ministers and educators that perhaps adult Negroes were rejecting their religious teaching because they preferred their own understandings.

Blacks greeted the religious instruction designed to free their souls without liberating their bodies with a conversion motif of their own, believing that once the soul was emancipated, the body also should be emancipated. Some slaves resented the message of docility preached by the missionaries and rejected it as "white man's religion," or religion that promised them spiritual freedom while keeping them in physical bondage. Other slaves complained that it was "hard for them to serve their earthly and heavenly masters."[29] But still others found meaning in the messages spread

73

by the plantation missionaries, accepted it on faith, and tried to incorporate it in their lives.[30]

Planters and slaveholders consistently dismissed the culture that Africans refused to give up completely as ignorant and barbaric. Yet each succeeding generation of Africans in America became more accustomed to Western culture and to the American way of doing things. However, black styles of speech, worship, and dress were still African. Even when Blacks sang the lyrics of European hymns, the music they sang had an African rhythm.

The bonding that occurred between missionaries and overseers contributed immensely to the effectiveness of rural evangelism. The overseer occupied a unique place in society. He was not on the same social level as the master of the plantation and was not in the class of landless, poor Whites from which he generally sprang, but occupied an uncertain position somewhere between the extremes.[31] In discharging their duties, ministers were expected to win the confidence and respect of the overseers who supervised the slave community. Ministers for the slaves were exhorted to treat overseers with respect: "Poor people have feelings as well as rich people, and if people are ignorant, yet they do not like to be told of it."[32]

The conversionist motif was fluid and flexible, changing as circumstances demanded to accommodate the social and racial climate at a particular time. But in spite of persecution and seemingly insurmountable impediments, black churches and black preachers managed to survive. In fact, many of the early urban black churches were not dependent on white churches at all for financial support. In Virginia, several African church choirs gave concerts and organized fairs to raise money for their churches. These churches provided help to their members and to the communities by burying the dead, comforting the bereaved, praying for the sick, and establishing benevolence funds to assist with daily necessities. In spite of obstacles, however, the proponents of instruction for Blacks argued that the gospel would enhance the moral and economic value of slaves: "To teach the practical points of morality—as honesty, sobriety, chastity, and industry— would not only improve the slave, but would tremendously enhance his economic value."[33] Before the end of the 1830s, the indifference and hostility of earlier generations gave way to the willing and ever increasing activity of the master to secure religious instruction for his Negroes.

After the major denominations had divided over slavery and the lines were clearly defined between slaveholding states and nonslaveholding regions, Southerners again favored the earlier conversionist language that assumed that through acculturation and assimilation, Blacks could improve their situations. Many Southerners rationalized that improving the religious conditions of slaves would have a positive effect on the image and social and economic well-being of the whole southern region.

In the *Southern Christian Advocate*, William Capers, the first superintendent and chief exponent of plantation missions, gave the following vivid description of the work missionaries undertook the oral religious instructions of slaves:

> There sounds the bell in the belfry of the Negro mission. . . . But let us enter; the congregation has assembled, all in clean, though coarse apparel; here are the children, too, on the front benches. We pass over the straw-carpeted floor, and enter a new pulpit formed from the drapery of the oak and pine—the moss is twisted and wound 'round upright posts, enclosing a space large enough to stand in, and festoons of moss hung in front with cord and tassel attached, the latter formed by the burr of the pine. . . . The missionary rises, the Negroes follow his example and repeat after him the Apostles' Creed. Explanatory questions are then asked and readily answered, the Commandments are then repeated, a portion of the Scripture read and explained, a hymn sung and prayer offered, after which the sermon is delivered.[34]

The South employed its best minds to carve out a place for Blacks in a society that would improve the conditions of their lives without changing their state. Charles C. Jones and William Capers, two leading theoreticians, authored catechisms in a conversionist language, which reflected the fragility of society in the antebellum South and the difficult assignment of interpreting a liberating gospel to an enslaved people.

Both Jones and Capers introduced their catechisms with hymns, prayers, commandments, the Creeds, portions of

Scripture, and a section delineating the duties of husbands and wives, parents and children, masters and servants. It was the duty of the church to arrange religious teaching for all members of the masters' households, including the slaves. Under the heading "Duty of Masters," the church cited scripture such as "Masters give unto your servants that which is just and equal, knowing that ye also have a Master in heaven."[35] Under the heading "Duty of Servants," citations were principally drawn from letters of Paul: "Servants be obedient to them that are your masters."[36] The catechism further stated:

> It is the duty of Masters to *provide* for their Servants, both old and young, good houses, comfortable clothing, wholesome and abundant food; to take care of them when old, and infirm and crippled and useless; nurse them carefully in their sickness, and in nothing let them suffer, as far as their means will bear them out; and *keep their families together.* It is their duty to protect their Servants, from abuse or ill-treatment, and have justice done them when they are wronged. They are their Fathers and Guardians; Servants are members of their households.[37]

As for the slaves, the catechism enjoined them to

> count their masters "worthy of all honor," as those whom God has placed over them in this world; *"with all fear,"* they are to be *"subject to them,"* and obey them in all *things,* possible and lawful, with good will, and endeavor to *please them well,* . . . and let Servants serve their masters as faithfully behind their backs as before their faces. God is present to see, if their masters are not. Should they fall into the hands of hard and unjust and unequal masters, and *suffer wrongfully,* their course according to divine command is to *take it patiently,* referring their case to God; looking to him for support in their trials, and for rewards for their patience. And the Lord will surely remember them.[38]

Religious activities among slaves gave them greater freedom to express their talents than was ordinarily allowed. There were opportunities, within limits, for self-expression. A converted, truly born-again Christian was expected to witness and have a story to tell. Some slaves took full advantage of the expectation by testifying in prayer meetings and Methodist love-feasts. At most religious gatherings, Blacks enthusiastically proclaimed their faith through hymns. They were sometimes called on to pray, and a few participated in the governance of the church. Some slaves responded to the call to preach and exhort. Sometimes their first and only message was a testimony of their conversion experience.

Many slaves never completely conformed to the European-American style of worship. Overwrought Blacks were prone to blurt out interjections during preaching and prayer, though such outbursts were by no means limited to Blacks and were often encouraged by evangelical preachers. This is another example of the ways in which Africans had an impact upon the European-American style of worship.

Mason Crum began the chapter on plantation missions in his book, *Gullah: Negro Life in the Carolina Sea Island*, with these lines:

> The preacher reads the hymn divine,
> And we remember not a line,
>   But sing right on;
> And with the text we start to shout,
> Forgetting shame, or pride or doubt,
>   To heaven most gone.[39]

For many black people, the church, whether the visible or invisible institution, continued to be a citadel of hope for those on the brink of despair. Their emotional catharsis in worship was important because it served as a defense and survival mechanism. Religion provided slaves the hope of being free, even if that freedom was only a spiritual freedom.

Prior to the Revolutionary War, black preachers were allowed to exhort, but by the end of the eighteenth century, laws were passed that prohibited Blacks from traveling about to preach, for fear they were using their calling to spread the ideas of freedom and liberation. After the slaveholders became suspicious of black preachers, the denominations assigned white pastors to serve Blacks and Whites worshiping together in the same church. However, by the mid–nineteenth century, the act of Blacks and Whites worshiping together in the same church gradually was superseded by special services for Negroes held after the regular morning service or on Sunday afternoon.[40]

Blacks were gradually assigned leadership roles in the segregated churches, assisting white ministers in serving the black members of their congregations. Sometimes these black congregants were called deacons and occasionally were called on to serve the elements of communion to blacks parishioners. However, regardless of their titles or methods of election, Negro assistants had no standing in a church governed entirely by Whites.[41] Along with restrictions placed upon black members of mixed churches, there was a growing sentiment among white slaveholders for Blacks to worship in separate buildings under the supervision of a white minister. The church, under the influence of various usages of the conversionist language, was the first public institution both to integrate and to separate the races. The rationale for a separate congregation was to "bar congregations under the influence and control of ignorant . . . men."[42]

In many instances, church buildings were not large enough to accommodate the two groups. In addition, Whites were intimidated when large numbers of Blacks attended their churches. After Blacks began to worship in separate facilities, a few Whites were added to the congregation to manage the temporal affairs of the church, which included the trusteeship of the property. Slaves themselves were chattel and therefore forbidden to own property.

New birth was the primary qualification for Blacks and Whites to be members of the church. The same spirit that called them out of darkness into the marvelous light of church membership also had the power to call the converted layman to preach, whether that person was black or white. Blacks frequently petitioned the white-controlled denominations for license to enter Christian ministry. This presented the church with another problem: Recognizing and ordaining black clergy would not be in keeping with the church's commitment to keep all Blacks in a subordinate position perpetually. Yet, evangelical Christianity strongly endorsed the belief that God called particular persons to proclaim the gospel. The call by God was considered a divine imperative. Consequently, many black slaves that acknowledged their call insisted on preaching regardless of the outcome of the petition, even if it meant persecution or death. One tenacious black preacher was whipped for obeying God rather than humanity: He "held up his hands and told his persecutors, that he rejoiced not only to be whipped, but *would freely suffer death for the cause of Jesus Christ";* he averred that cutting off his head was the only effectual means of silencing him. Though the matter was not one about which all white churchmen agreed, a substantial number must have reasoned like the Reverend Charles Colcock Jones, of Liberty County, Georgia. Jones did not "see, if we take the word of God for our guide, how we can consistently exclude an entire people from access to the Gospel ministry, as it may please Almighty God from time to time, as he unquestionably does, to call some of them to it 'as Aaron was.'"[43]

In biracial churches, Negroes were listed on the membership rolls designated as branches or arms of churches.[44] This special category was used to show that black membership functioned as a separate unit but was subject to the control of the white parent body. Frequently, Negro missions or chapels were adopted by one or more predominantly white churches and were given white pastors as overseers. Another way of forming independent black churches with white supervision was to assign white missionaries to all-black congregations. These independent black missions had a degree of autonomy, but their ecclesiastical power rarely exceeded the parameters set by the white establishment.

Evangelical Christians, focusing on God's Word and personal testimony as the final authority on conversion, encouraged individual and institutional reform that also embraced the doctrine, "where the Spirit of the Lord is, there is freedom" (2 Cor. 3:17). The freedom inherent in Baptist polity accounts for much of the appeal of Blacks to the Baptist denomination. The church is where Blacks first learned the rudiments of administration and leadership and first experienced operating a business. In mixed churches and independent black churches supervised by Whites, Blacks served in advisory positions on some church committees. The limited opportunities and exposure given to Blacks in white churches provided them the leadership skills to successfully build their own independent churches after emancipation.[45] Consequently, independent black churches patterned their polity and church structure after the white churches to which they had been exposed.

One of the most celebrated and revered black pastors prior to the Civil War was Andrew Marshall, nephew of Andrew Bryan and Bryan's successor as pastor of Savannah First African Baptist Church. Marshall took over the reins as pastor in 1815, and by 1830, the congregation membership had grown to 2,417. His phenomenal success was interrupted when he permitted Alexander Campbell, a white traveling evangelist, to preach in his pulpit. Campbell espoused the idea that slavery was incompatible with the gospel, partly because Campbell thought that Marshall endorsed that same teaching. Violence erupted, causing Marshall and the majority of his congregation to be forcefully withdrawn from the church. The majority of the members supported Marshall because they realized that the white Baptist association, which controlled and held the deeds of independent black Baptist churches, was orchestrating the unrest in an effort to diminish Marshall's influence over his congregation and the black community.

Formal charges were filed before the Sunbury Baptist Association in 1832. A white Baptist committee investigated the allegations and recommended that Marshall be silenced for causing a schism in the church and be removed as pastor. After exhorting all faithful black Baptists to dissociate themselves from Marshall, the Association went on to resolve that "the [Savannah] First African Church, as a member of this Association, on account of its corrupt state be considered dissolved; and that measures be adopted to constitute a new [African] Church, as a branch of the [Savannah] White Baptist Church."[46] These drastic measures were coupled with a recommendation that the Second African Baptist Church and all African churches in the area be reconstituted as branches of white-controlled churches. The Association enjoined the civil authorities by transmitting copies of the resolutions to the mayor of Savannah and to the state legislature and by creating a special committee to interpret its actions to the secular arena. The Association sought approval of the white board of trustees, which held immediate legal jurisdiction over the property, to bar Marshall and his congregation from the premises. The Association argued that these measures were necessary to restore peace and happiness on behalf of black people. White Baptists recognized the power of Marshall's influence, and the Association lamented, "He has them so completely under control that they are ready on all occasions to sanction his mandates, whether right or wrong."[47] This fact did not please white Southerners. They wanted not only to diminish the influence of the northern abolitionists but also to stifle any type of black autonomy or leadership.

Marshall responded to the charges in a conciliatory manner. He sought the "aid and protection of the . . . [white controlled] Baptist Church of Savannah" and consented "to come under the supervision of the committee of [that church's] body."[48] Despite their cooperative spirit, black leaders would not agree to relinquish congregational autonomy voluntarily, but they agreed to dismiss Marshall. Meanwhile, as the negotiations dragged, Marshall remained the pastor of the church.[49]

Civil authorities refused to close the church, and the trustees of First African Church responded by attacking the right of the investigation committee to interfere with the affairs of an independent black Baptist church. The trustees also argued that the allegations against Marshall had not been proved. Finally in 1837, with Marshall still not deposed and after he had made two unsuccessful attempts to be readmitted into the Association, the Sunbury Baptist Association accepted his doctrinal pronouncement, which led to the reinstatement of both the pastor and the congregation.

Marshall's gifts of eloquent speaking and sound administration did not go unnoticed at home or abroad. One of his acquaintances said he was known in distant parts of the country and even across the Atlantic.[50] When dignitaries came to Savannah, they sought out the black pastor Marshall for a conference. Such luminaries as the Reverend George Lewis, an official of the Free Church of Scotland, and the Reverend I. Kirkpatrick of Charleston, a moderator of the Southern Presbyterian General Assembly, called on Marshall. Prominent tourists frequently attended regular Sunday services at First African Baptist Church. Eminent geologist Sir Charles Lyell attended one of Marshall's worship services and gave the following assessment of his worship experience: "A good sermon, scarcely, if at all, below the average standard of the compositions of white ministers. [His delivery is in] a fine sonorous voice in good style, and for the most part in good English."[51]

The Reverend John Overton Choules, pastor of Second Baptist Church in Rhode Island, spoke of Marshall's sermon as "great sweetness and power [more] than I have heard in any sermon for five years," and which Choules ranked among "the discourses of great men." He confessed that he knew of "no northern Doctor that [could] read [aloud] as well."[52] The Reverend John M. Krebs, pastor of Rutgers Street Presbyterian Church in New York City, was the most carried away by Marshall's sermon. Krebs attended a service that continued for almost two and a half hours, but he did not recall boredom or exhaustion during the service. What he remembered was that Marshall spoke "with clear articulation and with a strong voice" and rendered a sermon that had "a clear, full, consistent vein of thought running throughout the whole" but "was not for a moment deficient in force or devotion." Krebs was deeply touched by the "stirring Gospel eloquence" and sought out Marshall after the service. When meeting, Krebs and Marshall prayed that "it might be ours, with all the Israel of God, at our next probable meeting, to sit down . . . in the kingdom of God, at the marriage supper, when the Lamb Himself shall preside."[53]

Andrew Marshall once preached to the Georgia Legislature. In 1856, he visited New York City and preached at First Baptist Church and at other white churches. His scheduled appearances were announced in *The New York Daily Times*, in which his sermons were reported. On Marshall's return to his home in Savannah, he became critically ill in Richmond and was invited to convalesce at the home of the Reverend Basil Manley Jr., the president of Richmond Female College. Marshall died on December 8, 1856, apparently at the age of 101 after more than a month of confinement.[54]

The plantation missions were designed to counter the attack by abolitionists, to give the masters tighter control over their slaves, and to improve the moral and spiritual welfare of their slaves without altering their social status. Converting Blacks to Christianity signified that Whites recognized that Blacks had souls and minds, but the *judicious* religious teaching offered to them ensured that they would not be able to use religion or their minds to gain freedom from slavery. Obedience was foremost. Slaveholders wanted their slaves in mixed churches or in separate churches, but they were denied economic, social, and political equality in the major white denominations. The motive behind preaching to and teaching slaves was to make slaves content to be in an inferior state and to make them feel that God ordained their subordinate place in society and the church.

White planters, as well as white preachers, were skeptical of the outcome of their religious teaching to slaves. Charles Cotesworth Pinckney Jr. held this suspicion when he told the Charleston Agricultural Society in 1829 that "the exercise of religious prerogatives opened to slaves a sphere of freedom from white control."[55] When slaves were brought into the fellowship of the church, it was difficult to control their efforts toward autonomy, particularly when evangelical Christianity stressed new birth, personal intimacy with God, and knowing the Lord personally for himself or herself. Such an approach to religion will always foster individualism and independence. One principal idea surrounding the birth of Protestantism as it came to be interpreted in America was the priesthood of all believers, greater lay participation, corporate empowerment, and a more democratic governance of the temporal affairs of the church. Individual members could be involved in such matters as "calling" pastors, electing officers, disciplining members, and adding new members. As time passed, it became obvious to many that conversionist language was sending two conflicting messages. Slaves were hearing independence, and Whites were hearing control.

CHAPTER FOUR

Conversion and the Formation of the Colored Methodist Episcopal Church [1866–1870]

While much consideration has been devoted to the religious divergence and cultural separation of black and white religions, only scant attention has been given to the intimacy, interaction, cooperation, and accommodation between them. This chapter will focus on the Reconstruction politics surrounding the formation of the Colored Methodist Episcopal Church (CME Church), which involved cooperation, denominational competition, sectional rivalry, ecumenical outreach, interracial conflict, and negotiation for plantation mission properties. The purpose of this chapter is to take a detailed look at the various ways the northern Methodists (Methodist Episcopal Church, or MEC), southern Methodists (Methodist Episcopal Church South, or MECS), and African Methodists (African Methodist Episcopal Church, or AME, and African Methodist Episcopal Zion Church, or AMEZ) used the language of conversion to evangelize among the former slaves who remained with the MECS missions after the Civil War.

This chapter is limited to the role of conversion as a central feature in the formation of the CME Church. By examining this denomination, the reader should be able to draw inferences to better understand the emergence of other independent black denominations during the postemancipation period. For a complete and definitive study of the CME Church itself, consult Othal Hawthorne Lakey's *History of the CME Church*. William B. Gravely, Jennifer Judith Wojcikowski, and others also have made important contributions to the corpus of literature on the formation of the CME Church.

THE AFRICAN METHODIST EPISCOPAL CHURCH

The formation of the CME Church cannot properly be understood without having an awareness of the four options open to any Methodist freedperson. The churches mentioned above competed for the souls and loyalty of the former slaves. The first of these churches to be discussed, the AME Church, was founded in 1787 by Richard Allen in Philadelphia, Pennsylvania. While praying at the altar of St. George's Church, Richard Allen, Absalom Jones, William White, and Doris Ginnings were pulled from their knees by white members in order to make room for the white parishioners in the church. Allen and Jones led the black members in protest out of the church, and Allen purchased, with his own money, a blacksmith shop and held services there with his followers. Allen's congregation, Bethel Church, was not the only congregation formed because of northern discrimination.

Blacks in predominantly white congregations in the North were experiencing racial segregation and discrimination similar to what Allen and his followers had encountered at St. George's Church. It is ironic, in light of later history, to note that many early institutions to practice segregation were the churches of the North. In 1816, Blacks who attended churches in Philadelphia, Baltimore, and other communities and were subjugated to second-class status met with Richard Allen at the Bethel Church in

85

Philadelphia to establish the AME denomination. Yet, after Allen led his followers from St. George's Church, he continued to struggle to retain a relationship with the Philadelphia Conference of the Methodist Episcopal Church, and even after he organized the AME denomination. Examples of this ongoing discrimination include: Allen's followers, called "Allenites," threatened with expulsion from the Methodist Conference for soliciting donations in Philadelphia for building their own church; the Conference seeking to prevent the AME from using "Methodist" in its name; and after Allen incorporating his fledgling congregation into the Methodist Conference, the Conference taking over the church and assigning a white minister as pastor. Despite discrimination against his young congregation, Allen purchased an old black-smith shop for worship and moved it to his own property. Then he invited the white Methodist bishop Francis Asbury to dedicate his house of worship, named Bethel.

In short, black Christians in white congregations in Baltimore, Delaware, New York, and other northern cities shared a common experience of racial discrimination in mixed churches. Racism experienced in white churches inspired black Christians to call the first Black General Conference in April of 1816 and to organize the AME denomination and elect Bishop Allen as its first bishop. The AME Church became the first national African organization of any kind to be established in America, and today it is the largest black independent Methodist body.[1]

THE AFRICAN METHODIST EPISCOPAL ZION CHURCH

While the fledgling AME denomination was emerging in Philadelphia, ninety miles away in New York City, the African Methodist Episcopal Zion (AMEZ) Church was being born. The AMEZ Church, which is now the second largest black Methodist denomination, came into existence under a set of circumstances similar to that of the AME denomination. In 1796, Peter Williams, James Varick, George Collins, and Christopher Rush led African members out of St. John Street Methodist Church in

New York City in protest of the segregation and discrimination imposed on them by the white members. Varick, who was elected as the first AMEZ bishop, petitioned Bishop Francis Asbury of the Methodist Episcopal Church to let them hold their own church meetings with their own black preachers apart from the St. John Street Methodist Church. Bishop Asbury approved their request, and the AMEZ Church began separate worship services in 1796.[2]

THE METHODIST EPISCOPAL CHURCH

By the mid–nineteenth century, in addition to the separation of Blacks from the predominantly white churches (religious segregation), most of the white-controlled denominations, including the Methodist Episcopal Church, had divided over the controversial issues of slavery and abolition. The Methodist Episcopal Church (MEC), which is the matrix of American Methodism, organized on December 24, 1784 in Baltimore, Maryland, at the so-called Christmas Conference. Upon organization, the American Methodists adopted the antislavery stance of John Wesley, the founder of Methodism.

From the very inception of Methodism in America, the MEC enacted antislavery rules, but these rules were not enforced if they were found contrary to the rules of the states where the members resided. Therefore, the issue of slavery was left as a local issue. Each annual conference would construct its own rules about slavery. This denominational indecision led to a conflict between the antislavery forces in the North and proslavery constituents in the South. In the 1840s, this issue of slavery took center stage at the Quadrennial General Conferences. Hoping the problem would resolve itself, the denomination would neither condone nor condemn the practice of slavery, but their indecisiveness led to an exodus of members from the MEC between the 1840 General Conference and the next quadrennial session in 1844. By the latter date, denominational leaders were aware that the undecided issue of slavery was the problem. The dilemma was this: If the church failed to make a firm stand against slavery, it might lose members to a Wesleyan antislavery denomination, and if it made too strong a stand against slavery, the denomination might jeopardize the southern wing of the church.

The final dispute that led to the division of the MEC involved Bishop James O. Andrew of Georgia, who was a slave owner. To appease the antislavery faction, the conference voted to request that the bishop be removed from office if he did not manumit his slave property. After two weeks of debate, the conference voted that Bishop Andrew must desist from the exercise of his Episcopal office as long as he kept slaves.[3] Bishop Andrew did not emancipate his slaves, and the southern Methodist churches reacted in support of Bishop Andrew by withdrawing from the MEC.

THE METHODIST EPISCOPAL CHURCH SOUTH

One year after their departure from the MEC, in 1845, the southern Methodists organized the Methodist Episcopal Church South (MECS). The sectional division between the northern and southern Methodists lasted for eighty-five years and the two denominations did not reunite until 1939. After the division, the Methodist Episcopal Church South took primary responsibility for the physical, spiritual, and ideological protection of their slaves. The MEC did not play a direct role in the spiritual and physical welfare of Blacks in the South until after the Civil War.

Northerners maintained that the outcome of the Civil War had empowered them with the legal and moral authority to provide leadership for the conversion and restoration of the South. The assumed authority of the MEC did not convince the MECS, whose pastors continued to preach sermons and pray prayers that sustained a spirit of rebellion. Even though the North had won the Civil War, it did not win the allegiance of the defeated South. Northerners interpreted the outcome of the Civil War as divine providence that they should open the gates of the South to northern preachers and teachers in order to educate and save millions of ignorant and downtrodden human beings.[4] Since the MECS had been corrupted by the evils of slavery, according to northern churches, the MEC concluded that the South had forfeited its ability to convert and to facilitate restoration.[5]

THE WAR ENDS,
BUT RELIGIOUS STRUGGLE CONTINUES

The Evangelistic Efforts of the MEC

The goal of the northern evangelistic enterprise in the South was to convert and reclaim both Whites and Blacks. After the war, many Northerners viewed the South as a home mission field because they judged that slavery had ruined the moral fabric of southern society. Initially, Northerners devised a twofold plan to convince white Southerners to rejoin the MEC by evangelizing throughout the southern region and converting former slaves.[6] Many white Southerners considered the conversionist language and evangelistic approach of the MEC insulting and humiliating. Even after their defeat, Southerners did not readily relinquish the belief that the South was still their sacred domain. They remained independent in soul even after the conclusion of their physical rebellion. The evangelistic efforts of the MEC merely fanned the fire of hatred and bitterness still smoldering from the defeat of the war. After its evangelistic plan failed to convert white southerners, the MEC continued to convert Blacks. However, the MEC was divided over the evangelistic strategy to appeal to black converts. Some members of the MEC concluded that the most effective method of evangelizing would be to encourage Blacks to organize their own separate churches, but the majority saw the end of the war as an opportunity to add more Blacks to existing membership rolls.[7]

MECS leaders, even after the war, continued to rationalize that the conflict between them and the MEC revolved around fundamental differences in their perceptions of the role of the church in society. And Southerners resented the fact that Northerners believed the Civil War had been fought primarily for the emancipation of slaves. Southerners had maintained that slaves were property under the domain of civil authority and not under church authority. The outcome of the war did not change their outlook; they still thought it both immoral and illegal for northern abolitionists to interfere with southern slave property.

Even after the South had been defeated, this hostile spirit did not change. War ceased, and the Emancipation Proclamation was enforced, but the controversy, bickering, wrangling, and disputes were long from over. One of the most costly and lasting results of the Civil War was its legacy of sectional hatred and resentment between the North and the South. After the North had won the war, northern civil and religious authorities assumed that it was their mission to reconstruct the South not only religiously but also politically and socially. But the religious entanglements resulting from the war were no less confusing than the political and social entanglements. Religious reconstruction was as contested an issue as political reconstruction.

The South accused the North of preaching an extraneous gospel because many northern churches had "incorporated social dogmas and political tests into their church creeds."[8] Retaining the argument that slavery had not caused the war, many southerners concluded that the removal of slavery would not restore the Union. Southern church members argued that they had fought the war to protect their region from northern apostasy and heretical doctrine. These theological and sectional differences, reflected in the division between the MECS and the MEC, regarding the role of the church in society, helped shape Northerners' and Southerners' respective conversionist language and evangelistic strategies.

The MECS lamented that the North had infringed upon their jurisdiction and enticed thousands of black members, or former slaves, to leave the southern denomination as part of the conversionist plan in the South. In fact, the number of black members reported at the beginning of the war had already diminished from 207,000 to 78,000 by the end of the war.[9] After the denomination witnessed a dramatic decline in membership, the major question confronting the 1866 General Conference of the MECS was what should be done to promote the religious interests of the African people.[10] Most of the black members who had defected from the MECS most likely transferred their memberships to the African Methodist Episcopal Church (AME Church), African Methodist

Episcopal Zion Church (AMEZ Church), or the MEC.[11] The exodus of black members required that the General Conference address the protection of the remnant of their black members from northern competitors.[12] But the appeal of white Southerners for black communicants to remain in their churches fell largely on unreceptive ears. Black Christians would no longer follow a Christianity that preached racially motivated subservience and white supremacy.

However, the decline of black membership in the MECS was not unique to Methodism. Many primarily white denominations experienced a mass defection of black members from their white-controlled churches. The experience of the First Baptist Church in Montgomery, Alabama, is one of many examples. In 1865, it reported six hundred black and three hundred white members. Black members petitioned the white-controlled church for their own religious body, and the First Baptist Church reluctantly granted their request.[13] Black Baptists, too, had their fill of white Christianity during slavery and its message of servitude.

The Evangelistic Efforts of the AME

The northern AME, which had been an independent black church for more than three quarters of a century, sent delegates to the 1866 General Conference of the MECS to compete for plantation mission property and for the souls of the former slaves of the southern Methodists. The AME representatives presented their request in conversion language with a keen sense of "divine precedence." They felt as if they had been divinely summoned for the "Christianization of the newly freed persons in order that [those persons] may become good citizens."[14] By tempering the conversionist language ("Christianization") with political ends ("that they may become good citizens"), the AME members sought to appease the MECS and prepare them for the AME bishop's request to transfer peaceably and permanently the mission properties to the authorities of the African Episcopal Church.[15]

Attempting to acquire property and convert black souls, AME delegates sought to create a bond between themselves and the MECS by recognizing their common heritage with Wesleyan Methodism. The AME founder, Bishop Allen, was one of only

91

two black delegates present at the Organizing General Conference of American Methodism in Baltimore in 1784. His denomination shared with the MEC church polity, liturgy, and theology. On racial matters, the AME Church shared the opinion of John Wesley, the founder of Methodism, who also opposed slavery. The delegates at the 1866 General Conference of the MECS made it perfectly clear that the AME Church was anxious to adopt and care for the spiritual needs of her black children by sending its bishops to negotiate the adoption and to encourage familial ties between the two denominations.[16] In spite of northern African Methodists' eagerness to be the guardians of black Methodists' souls and property, the General Conference would not transfer their properties to the AME denomination.

The MEC denomination was as determined as the AME Church to receive southern property, and the MECS was as much against giving the property to them as to the AME. However, the MECS did consider the AME Church a lesser threat to the southern denomination than the MEC. In order to shield Africans from the infidelity and republicanism of the northern Methodists, white Southerners encouraged black Methodists to join the AME churches rather than their northern counterparts, if Blacks intended to leave the MECS.[17] Consequently, the MECS endorsed a union with the AME only in order to impede the northern evangelistic efforts among southern Blacks. But Southerners were uncomfortable with either the white-controlled MEC or the black-controlled AME playing a significant role in charting the future of black southern Methodists. Many white Southerners feared that white and black Northerners would encourage freedpersons to push for full societal equality.[18] The fear that black members would be pulled into politics was the primary reason the MECS was skeptical about turning properties over to the AME.[19]

The AME representative may have anticipated the lukewarm response of the MECS to the AME's property request but may have been less prepared for the opposition received from the black members of the MECS. When the AME and white MEC members journeyed south to evangelize among the former slaves, they failed to grasp the difficulty former slaves experienced in severing their emotional ties to the MECS. After emancipation, one black Methodist preacher in Griffin, Georgia, who serves as an excellent example of the Africans' sentiment, was invited to leave the MECS for the MEC. The former slave preacher responded with a resounding, "No, I have never been persuaded to leave my church, for when I was on the way to ruin she took me in her arms and pointed me to the Lamb of God that taketh away the sins of the world."[20]

Since the acquisition of property had been a driving force and the hidden agenda in the AME's use of conversionist language—an interest in evangelizing that was much the same for the black members of the MECS—the ridicule and stereotyping by AME members of Blacks who remained with the MECS was unjustifiable. After the evangelistic appeals of the AME failed, some sarcastically called the black members of the MECS "Democrats," "bootlicks," and "white folks' niggers."[21]

The MECS's determination to "protect" its black membership and, at the same time, to leave the door open for the AME to unite with them shaped the evangelistic work of the MECS among Blacks. For example, the legislative body of the 1866 conference adopted a threefold plan of action, or evangelistic strategy: (1) to create separate charges and annual conferences within the MECS for black members, (2) to refuse transfer of property to the AME, but, at the same time, (3) to open dialogue on a union with the AME while working out accommodations for the use of property at the local church level.[22] In return for using the MECS property, the AME would not seek to divide the MECS black missions or "induce [the black members] to leave [the missions]," and the MECS would not prevent their former slaves, potential AME members, from leaving when of their own motion, they prefer to do so.[23] The MECS crafted this plan hoping it would protect and retain their remaining black members and prevent remaining Blacks from leaving the denomination.

A NEW BLACK DENOMINATION: FORMATION OF THE COLORED METHODIST EPISCOPAL CHURCH

Black Methodists were formerly enslaved by white Southerners but were nevertheless determined to build on their existing relationship with the white-controlled MECS. Fearing that more Blacks might desert the church, white Methodists encouraged Blacks to evangelize among their own people and to work out their own destinies. From 1866 through 1869, these former slaves were supported and encouraged by the MECS to evangelize and organize their people into local congregations and conferences. The phenomenal success of preemancipated leaders encouraged freedpersons to seek ecclesiastical autonomy and proved that Blacks were not inherently inferior. These early leaders proved that if given the opportunity, they could administer their own affairs. Yet while black members had an independent organization, they remained within the church.[24] White members would still legislate and administer the discipline of the church for them, but black members would function as an independent track of the MECS.[25]

These freed black Methodists, though they remained independent and with the MECS, were dissatisfied with their inferior status among the majority-white churches. Leaders of postemancipated black Methodism diplomatically negotiated for their ecclesiastical identity and expressed their dissatisfaction by petitioning the MECS for their own independent denomination. The Colored Methodist Episcopal Church (the CME Church, now the Christian Methodist Episcopal Church), a result of this push for independence, was one of the first national African-American organizations to form in the postemancipation era.

The CME Church was conceived and delivered during the Reconstruction era. Southern Blacks and Whites used the language of conversion to protect their vested interests in the formation of the new denomination. The MECS wanted to continue a paternalistic relationship with their former slaves in order to diminish the influences of the more radical MEC and AME denominations. And black members saw an opportunity to have their own denomination, with indigenous clergy and lay leadership. The white MECS had considered establishing a black general conference, but black members would have remained under the jurisdiction of the white MECS bishops. This was unacceptable to black leaders who reasoned that with a black bishop to preside, they should go among their people with a hope not indulged this far."[26]

The MECS white missionaries were serious, and many felt divinely called to minister to the spiritual welfare of their former slaves. The eminent scholar Donald G. Mathews, in his book *Religion in the Old South,* maintained that "the gospel of love could sometimes be mistaken as a means instead of an end; the conversion of slaves became the means of saving the South."[27]

As we have already seen in previous chapters, Blacks and Whites were the products of an interdependent culture, religion, and plantation system they had built together. They ate the same food, prepared by the same cooks; many were nursed by the same nannies. They attended the same revivals, and many Blacks and Whites were converted by the same preachers. In addition to their having one heavenly Father, many had the same earthly father. The new birth experience was a crucial event in the lives of many people of both races. For many former slaves, the conversion experience provided them with their first sense of belonging to a community. Their conversion was synonymous with being born into the family of God.

In contrast to the birth of the AME (and AMEZ), the origin of the CME was quieter and less dramatic but no less significant. The CME came into existence under different circumstances, but the circumstances were no less committed to freedom and self-determination—the same impetus that led to the genesis of the AME (and AMEZ) nearly a century earlier.

Though the 1866 plan to evangelize and organize Blacks could be perceived as a desperate grasp for control by the MECS in an increasingly uncontrollable situation, future CME leaders embraced it as an opportunity for educational and ecclesiastical advancement and community building. During 1866, the transfer of ecclesiastical power from the white church to members of the black community commenced as the annual conferences began ordaining black preachers. Listed in the annual conference minister directories with the designation "col'd" next to their names, these men were selected by white quarterly conferences and confirmed by a vote from white annual conferences. By the end of 1866, the annual conferences of the white Methodist Episcopal Church South had ordained twenty-six black local preachers and two black presiding elders.[28]

Religious independence and economic empowerment were priorities for the future members of the CME. They wanted control over their own religious affairs, and they felt they were the legitimate heirs of the property from the plantation missions. These black Methodists did not want to lose their previously established relationships nor the amenities that could accrue to them if they were to fraternize with AME members. The MECS welcomed the opportunity to organize Blacks into a church of their own, "whereas the Northern [Methodists were] strenuously urging [southern Blacks] to join their congregations."[29] Also, the southern black Methodists' regional ties with the MECS were stronger than their ethnic affinity with AME members. From the point of view of these southern black Methodists, it was more advantageous to be an ally of the former slave owners than to form an alliance with the AME: "The African Methodist Episcopal Church [has] done nothing for us, while the MECS is willing to assist us in establishing our own independent church organization."[30] In short, the transfer of the property to these southern black Methodists may be interpreted as a kind of spiritual reparation for their free labor.

Future CME members embraced their region by distinguishing themselves from both the AME and the MEC. Freedmen often denounced the AME as "Caesar's men," who had gone to the South only to swell their membership rolls while acquiring mission properties from the MECS, who regarded themselves (for whom region mattered) as spiritual people, and who had separated from regional politics.[31] The future CME members were frequently ridiculed and criticized for their conservative position. In response to the charge that, for example, the Reverend Sandy Kendall, a presiding elder in the Georgia Colored Conference, was "hired by white people to stay with them," Kendall would argue vehemently that he was "called" by God "to preach the gospel at all times and at all places."[32] A report by one AME missionary provides a graphic description of some future CME church members' unwillingness to unite with their northern brothers and sisters: "They rather have 'one of our own men' though he be a nincompoop and know nothing of a Boston, New York, or Philadelphia training in school teaching, nor has [he] ever even rubbed . . . against a College wall, than an intelligent Northerner or foreigner."[33] Many CME members may have concurred with the sentiment that AME church members (missionaries and evangelists) were "manipulative Yankees."[34]

The leaders of what became the CME denomination diplomatically employed a conversionist language compatible with the white Southerners' views of the role of the church in society. Lucius Holsey, gifted offspring of the plantation missions and major player in the organizing mission conference, which led to the formation of the CME, clearly articulated the position of the white Southerners of the MECS when he maintained that "Christianity . . . should remain aloof from politics, not as individuals, but as representatives of the churches."[35]

By not overtly opposing the paternalism of white Southerners, these future members of the CME were rewarded with church property and protection from the persecution and opposition of the AME and MEC. To enhance his relationships with white ministers and to solidify patronage, the southern black Methodist itinerant Sandy Kendall illustrated his determination not to be swayed by the AME. He wrote: "They begged me not to stay in the old church, but never will I forget my obligation to the church, and my duty as her representative among colored people." In spite of the "diverse temptation and cross pulling on every side, he managed to hold out faithful to the end."[36]

From 1867 to 1869, AME missionaries filled the pages of the *Christian Recorder* with complaints regarding southern black preachers who continually blocked their efforts. For example, Theophilus Gould Steward, an AME missionary, lamented that upon his arrival at the predominantly black Methodist Episcopal Church in Lumpkin, Georgia, the Reverend William Crayton was "not at all pleased at being supplanted." He came into conflict with the southern black itinerant Crayton, whom Steward described as "very poorly equipped for his task."[37] Steward's efforts to organize the members of the Lumpkin church into an AME congregation were greeted with Crayton's and the church members' stringent opposition, which grew increasingly "bitter and fierce."[38]

Though Steward eventually won possession of that particular

church, many other AME missionaries faced ministers and church members who were unwilling to acquiesce to the AME Church. For example, the Reverend Edward West of the Georgia Colored Conference, who fought to keep the black (MECS) mission in Augusta from joining AME churches, was ordained presiding elder of the Georgia Conference in 1866. West also ministered to the predominantly black congregation in Augusta's Trinity Church: "A large sumptuous edifice with an immense congregation of people and hundreds of members, Trinity was an attractive ecclesiastical acquisition."[39]

The AME first encountered West in Augusta in the summer of 1865. Upon his arrival in that city, the Reverend James Lynch met with West, whom Lynch described as "a very respectable minister" of the MECS.[40] By the winter of 1866, the opinion of some of the members of the AME regarding West had changed dramatically. In a letter to the *Recorder*, the Reverend Henry M. Turner bitterly referred to West as a "rebel" and "old and ignorant."[41]

The praise of West changed when he resisted the AME Church's missionary intrusions into MECS-controlled black missions. Reporting from the Georgia mission field in 1866, Reverend Turner wrote that although most churches were headed "in the right direction," Trinity Church had not left the MECS "The only one who keeps it there," bemoaned Turner, "is Reverend Edward West."[42] In 1867, AME missionaries characterized West's rivalry as "far more aggravating" than any other incident they had encountered.[43] Though the majority of the southern black churches throughout Georgia had joined the AME church, Trinity Church, under the influence of West, was unwavering in its loyalty to the MECS.

The intraracial conflict was strongest among those black Methodists who had left the MECS for the AME only to return when white southern churches granted black members a separate ecclesiastical structure. Three of the first five bishops of the soon-to-be-organized CME church had left the MECS for the AME and reunited with the white Southern Methodist Church when the MECS finally provided black members with these independent ecclesiastical structures. The lure that drew these ministers back to the MECS (or rather, to the CME) was most likely the resources made available by white Southerners to Blacks to evangelize their own people in order to establish an independent denomination. These former AME ministers, who rejoined the MECS, presented the most formidable opposition to the intrusion of the AME into the future plantation missions.

The case of the Reverend William Campbell, who was at first a member of the MECS, then a member of the AME, and then a returning member of the MECS, illustrates the fierce rivalries between the black members of the MECS and the members of the AME over land and church buildings. In 1866, the Georgia Conference of the AME Church ordained Campbell elder in Savannah "in the emergency ministry" created to fill the southern mission's ministerial needs. However, in 1868, Campbell was attracted to the evangelistic opportunities provided by the white MECS, and he led a "conspiracy to draw off members and set up a rival congregation."[44]

Campbell bargained his joining the MECS by promising to form their black mission with his Sunday school of two hundred and thirty-nine children. This action prompted a counterattack by the Reverend Steward, who interrupted Campbell's service the next Sunday morning and announced that he would organize an AME Sunday school. Campbell lost the majority of his Sunday school pupils to Steward, but the incident solidified his support of the MECS in its efforts to evangelize and organize black members. The AME Church's "turncoat" Campbell was ordained deacon and elder in the MECS by Bishop George F. Pierce, and Campbell, armed with a letter from the trustees of the MECS, ordered Steward to surrender a church building in Savannah, Georgia, "for the newly organized colored body comprised of secedes from our congregation."[45] Arguing over the rightful owners of the property continued until, on February 17, 1869, the night before the AME congregation was to hand over the keys, the church suspiciously burned to the ground.[46]

First Steps: The Creation of "Colored" Conferences

By the beginning of 1869, from the shadows of the plantation, white preachers, such as James Evans and Samuel Watson, and white bishops and black preachers organized black Methodists into conferences within the MECS in Tennessee, Kentucky, Mississippi, Georgia, and Alabama. The MECS denomination provided the model that the black Methodists used to fashion the new church. The form of government and beliefs were similar to those of other black independent Methodist denominations, which meant that race, and not differences in theology or polity, was the major issue that divided the Methodist family. The southern white bishops of the respective conferences stated that they were impressed with the character and ability of the early leaders. For example, while supervising the first black MECS Georgia Conference, Bishop George F. Pierce noted the rapidity with which black members learned the polity and administrative structure of the Methodists. Like Pierce, Bishop Holland McTyeire of Kentucky reported that black Methodists in "the quarterly and annual conferences . . . are having development and learning how to work the machinery."[47]

The black Methodists petitioned the MECS to implement the plans set forth in the 1866 General Conference for the formation of a separate denomination for black members. "Through letters, memorials, and annual conference proceedings, these leaders argued that they should be granted their own General Conference on the grounds of their proven fidelity as southern Methodists, their demonstrated ability as itinerant ministers, and their potential [ability] as racial mediators."[48]

Many black leaders used a language of conversion that appealed to white Southerners' interests and benefits if they assisted black MECS members in forming a separate denomination. They bargained with the MECS, reminding white members that if they did not cooperate with the efforts of black MECS ministers, they would alienate and lose even more black members.[49] Also, black ministers pointed out that they could promote peace and harmony between the races and diminish the influence of the radical politics from the northern churches.[50] This could be achieved by building on the relationship the MECS had with Blacks before emancipation. The black leaders impressed upon the white MECS that they had a rapport with the people in the region and were best equipped to organize churches and annual conferences for the proposed separate black denomination.

The early pioneers of the soon-to-be formed CME used the

annual conference structure of the MECS as a platform to promote their movement for an independent and separate denomination. On January 4, 1869, sixty black preachers joined by black lay members gathered with Bishop Pierce to form the first annual Georgia Colored Conference.[51] In giving account of their stewardship, the black itinerants reported over twelve hundred members in their charges. After Bishop Pierce had ordained seventeen deacons and fourteen elders, he said that the character and intelligence of the black members present exceeded the expectations of all white members present.[52] Pierce also remarked that the "conference was well attended and [that] their singing was inspiring. They sang with the spirit and there were 1000 copies of the minutes."[53] The reporting of 1000 copies of the minutes is noteworthy because one of the proud traditions of the CME has been its emphasis on literacy and education. According to C. Eric Lincoln and Lawrence H. Mamiya, the CME has the highest percentage among the seven mainline black denominations of clergy that have attended graduate school.[54]

The conference convened at Trinity Church in Augusta, the church that Edward West had fought to keep out of the hands and control of the AME. Here, black leaders, including the Reverends Lucius Holsey, Richard Vanderhorst, and Isaac Anderson, pressured Bishop Pierce for his support at the 1870 MECS Conference, where they planned to petition the white church for complete independence.

Petitioning for an Independent General Conference[55]

Bishop Pierce agreed with the black ministers' request for an autonomous denomination but did not concur with the urgency. "The ball is in motion," Pierce contended, but black members, in Pierce's opinion, were not yet ready to "stand alone."[56] White Southerners were reluctant to relinquish their paternalistic control, and Pierce lamented that his greatest fear was that black MECS members would "haste[n] consummation of their independence."[57] The southern Methodist bishop attributed the black MECS ministers' impatience to an "outside pressure [that] hastened their need for an independent jurisdiction."[58]

Bishop Pierce was tremendously impressed with the black

itinerants of the Georgia Conference. Pierce reported that during deliberation the conference used the normal parliamentary rules in Methodist polity. Not only that, as the following anecdote shows, he appreciated their excellent judgment and well-employed sense of humor: Bishop Pierce said he asked one of the black preachers if he had a recommendation for an appointment. The black preacher replied, "No, Sir, I am done recommending preachers." "Why?" "I come across one not long ago. I thought he was nice and smart . . . I told the people what a promising man he was and he got up to preach and told the congregation that the Lord ordained Jonah to go to Connecticut and he went off to Arkansas or Texas." He said, "Since then I quit recommending preachers."[59]

Bishop McTyeire also received pressure from the black members of the Kentucky MECS conference and shared the conservative sentiments of his colleagues. "Some would have a general conference next year," he reported, "but [Pierce] advised them not to move 'too fast.'"[60] Nevertheless, black leaders attending the 1870 MECS general conference petitioned the legislative body to assist them in "perfecting" their own separate denomination.[61] Representatives from the Tennessee Colored Conference of the MECS presented a petition in conversionist language that urged the white church to move expeditiously in granting ecclesiastical independence. They insisted that the time had come for a general conference to be "organized for [their] race."[62] During the discussion that ensued, white southern Methodists in attendance conceded that many of their black members had left the church after the war because they did not know that a separate church would be organized. The black members of the MECS advised the conference delegates, "In order that there be no alienation on the part of our people, we ask that you form at once and authorize the organization of a colored general conference."[63]

The Reverend Theophilus Gould Steward, a black representative to the general conference, solicited the cooperation, prayers, and money of the white MECS members and took the initiative to offer a detailed plan for separation: "We would respectfully solicit your honorable body to appoint a delegation say five to meet . . . on the 16th day of December 1870 at Jackson, Tennessee, to confer with our delegates in organizing our contemplated colored general conference."[64] He also mentioned a list of four white ministers and one white lay member whom they wished to be appointed as delegates to the newly formed conference.[65] After considerable debate, the general conference adopted Steward's resolution in its entirety.

White southern Methodists voted to hold a black Methodist General Conference in the fall of 1870 to assist with the organization of black members into a separate denomination. White Bishops Robert Paine and McTyeire were delegated the responsibility of overseeing the organizing conference. The MECS was "compelled" by black Methodists' actions and the force of their arguments "to take the course of action to meet the demands even though many of the wisest heads in that body deemed the notion premature and would have postponed the separation."[66] Feeling that the white Southerners were indebted to them for their labor and loyalty, the pioneers of the soon-to-be-formed CME Church insisted that their former masters owed them support and financial resources in organizing an independent church, and they were deliberate and intentional in their request for support.

The MECS was reluctant to relinquish properties designated for black mission worship houses to anyone, even to those Blacks who had remained loyal to the denomination. The MECS would have preferred keeping black members in a subordinate status and retaining control of their souls and the property, but the formation of a separate denomination was underway and could not be halted. After protracted debate over the use and transfer of property, white members acceded to the request by instructing those in charge to transfer property titles to the properly constituted trustees of the future CME. However, white Southerners, in transferring the property, made stipulations to ensure that the northern churches would not control or interfere with southern churches. They warned the black communicants not to forget the property by entangling with political churches.[67] One white MECS member clarified the denomination's position on further avoiding alienating southern blacks:

Do not misunderstand me. It is to be expected, and it is proper, that every man have his political opinions. . . . And it is to be expected, that members of the Church take part in public political matters. And Christianity does not require any man to abstain from . . . politics. . . . But the courthouse or the public hall, and not the church is the place for these things. As the minister of Christ is the gospel to all, he should abstain from political agitation both public and private.[68]

A "Colored" General Conference

On December 16, 1870, five years removed from human bondage, forty-one clerical and lay delegates from eight conferences convened in Jackson, Tennessee, to constitute the Colored Methodist Episcopal (now known as the Christian Methodist Episcopal) denomination. These unlettered but undaunted men were advised by white MECS bishops, but they also debated and questioned the counsel and canon of the white southern Methodist denomination. They paid particular attention to matters critical to members' welfare. For example, the black delegates debated educational requirements for their ministers and adopted ministerial requirements suitable to their particular situation. The white MECS required ministers who applied for local preachers' licenses to evidence "knowledge of the ordinary branches of an English education."[69] The early leaders of the new black denomination were fully aware of the importance of education, but they were also painfully aware of the legacy of slavery, which denied blacks the basic rudiments of literacy. Neither were they so naive as to think that these shortcomings had been overcome in only five years. To accommodate ministers who had no formal training, some of the black delegates advocated a more lenient education requirement than the one mandated for clergy by the white-dominated MECS. One black delegate proposed that the prospective licentiate evidence the ability to "read the word of God."[70] This proposal ignited fiery debate among the delegates. For example, on the one hand, Anderson Jackson of Alabama strongly opposed any educational requirements for preaching the gospel: "It ain't for us, brethrin', to measure out a man by a book, and say who God shall call and whom he shan't. My father, sir, didn't know A and B, and yet by his preaching hundreds—yes thousands—was converted. Scores of [those] in heaven, now, white as well as black."[71] William Miles of Kentucky, on the other hand, argued that some educational requirements for ministry were important to the welfare and continued improvement of the newly freed congregations:

> The past must go for itself. We have new duties, and must get ready for them. What are you going to do with all those children who are [now] in school? [Have] them taught to read, and then send men to preach to them that can't read? Shut up your schools to keep your congregation level with the pulpit, or raise your pulpit to keep it level with your congregation.[72]

Miles's persuasive argument prevailed, and a minimal educational requirement for ministers was established. Miles and the conference had set the stage for the CME's legacy of trained clergy and support for educational institutions. These pioneers in black Methodism thus affirmed with far-reaching vision that conversion for the CME would include a rebirth and revival of persons in body, soul, and *mind*.

One of the most critical issues confronting the new denomination was its name. The unique importance of changes in the nomenclature used to identify African Americans and their institutions over against other ethnic groups, often accompanying metamorphoses in social and cultural location, can be seen in W. E. B. DuBois's coinage of the term dialectical "double-consciousness."[73] As and example of such, the naming of the new denomination headed the agenda for the committee on organization. The committee was chaired by the talented Isaac Anderson from Georgia. Anderson, who knew the rudiments of parliamentary procedure, was not exactly a novice in this role. He had also been a member of the Constitutional Convention of Georgia, which had revised the document for Georgia's readmission to the union. Anderson and other remarkably talented freed persons on the committee worked to present the General Conference with an appropriate name for the new denomination.

The black delegation from Winchester, Kentucky, had come to the 1870 Organizing General Conference prepared with a resolution insisting that the new denomination's name reflect the national posture of the church rather than of sectional politics.

Their resolution, couched in language regarding effective evangelism and conversion, read thus:

> Grace to you and peace from God, our Father, and the Lord Jesus Christ.
>
> We thank our God, through Jesus Christ, for you all, that our Church is widening its sphere of usefulness, and is gathering into its fold true and penitent believers; for we desire nothing so much as the spreading of the gospel of Christ. May your deliberations be guided by wisdom from on high: and, in your instituting a new order of things in our Church, our daily prayer shall be: "May the Lord direct you." If it be the will of God, our desire is that colored bishops be appointed or elected to take charge of and preside over the colored Church. It is our desire that our organization be known under the name of the "Methodist Episcopal Church"— not that we wish to sever our connection with the "Methodist Episcopal Church, South": not that we want to unite with the "Methodist Episcopal Church, North"; but as our Savior called us to come unto him, let us imitate his goodness and purity, and in name avoid all stumbling-blocks, and, looking heavenward, move on triumphantly to the prize of the high calling in Christ Jesus. Some of the churches in Central Kentucky have engendered some bitterness of feeling on this account; and this slight change would produce harmony and unity of action that would render us invincible against the hosts of this world, and perhaps would be the means of saving many a wearied and lost soul.[74]

Reflecting a diplomatic sophistication far beyond their five years of legal freedom, these freedpersons sought to distance their denomination from ridicule, especially from the aspersion that they had become pawns for the white-controlled MECS. The naming of the denomination, as pointed out above, was extremely important—vital—for a people who had been so systematically divested of name and identity. This sensitive issue, however, would not be so easily won. The Reverend James Evans, who had been authorized by the 1866 General Conference to help superintend the formation of the new denomination, contended that the name should be Colored Methodist Episcopal Church, South. Prior to organizing the General Conference, the white-controlled MECS, in their literature, referred to their black constituency using the name Evans argued should be made official, thus emphasizing the connection with the southern white-controlled denomination.

The black members of this formative convention, however, insisted that the name represent a clean break from the shadows of the plantation missions and from regional politics, by invoking the traditional name of original North American Methodism. The delegates to the Organizing General Conference of the CME resolved: "Whereas the Methodist Episcopal Church in America was the name first given to the Methodist church in the United States, we simply prefix the word 'colored' to the name, and for ourselves, adopt the name."[75] The leaders of the new denomination thus maintained that their ecclesiastical identity extended beyond the southern plantation into the unbroken tradition of early American Methodism.

However, the name "colored" evoked thoughts of the natal separation (alienation at birth) of Blacks from their African roots during slavery. The peculiar institution of slavery had been designed to strip Blacks of their indigenous culture, history, beliefs, and *names*. Consequently, when the leaders of the newly independent CME named their denomination, they did not insist on direct identification with Africa. Slavery had divested them of any thought of their claim to an African heritage. These black itinerants would even boast of their choice to distance themselves from Africa. Instead, they had embraced *American* Methodism. The Reverend Isaac Lane, a member of the Tennessee Colored Conference, remarked, "Other independent Negro Methodist churches had rebelled and seceded" and forfeited their place in the Methodist hierarchy of religious authority.[76] He was referring to the AME and connecting the reference to "African" in its name with rebellion against the duly established American Methodist churches. But it was, of course, the legacy of slavery that had denied these "colored" Methodists their African name.

Even before they were able to give full expression to their identity, however, their African ancestors sang the spiritual, "Hush! Somebody's Calling My Name."[77] Like many spirituals, "Hush, Somebody's Calling My Name" has several meanings. Since the slaves had been denied their African names—names such as Kenyatta, Jaba, Cuffy, Abba, and Seth—in silence (Hush), they could still hear somebody calling their African names. After conversion, slaves looked on themselves as having two masters—one on earth and one in heaven. Conversion provided them with a new identity (in the image of God) and a new name.

These black Methodists—as we have seen in chapters 1–3—were products of an environment that had systematically prevented slaves from integrating the experiences and memory of their African ancestors into their present existence. They were former slaves, the descendants of people who had been ruthlessly uprooted from Africa and alienated from all formal ties of blood, from all localities or groups other than those chosen by their masters. The founding leaders of the CME Church did not embrace assimilating with the African Methodists for two reasons: First, the CME Church members were determined to build their lives, churches, schools, and families on the relationships they had cultivated with the MECS prior to emancipation. And, second, the process of natal separation imposed on them by the institution of slavery had severed the "umbilical cord" of blood ties to African heritage, ancestry, history, and even an appreciation for African culture.

The first generation of slaves had clung tenaciously to their African names. Living under rules of slavery that prohibited slaves from using African names, Blacks used their Anglo names when dealing with white people and their African names when in conversation with other Blacks. During this early period of slavery, it was a badge of honor to be called by an African name. The early independent black churches and organizations also had "African" affixed to their names. However, with the passing of time, succeeding generations became more acculturated to American life and alienated from their African past. In short, the racial designation "colored" in the name of the new denomination was also an insidious remnant of the systematic natal separation of African Americans.

Perfecting the Conference: The Seating of Black Bishops

The zenith of one of the most momentous gatherings in American black church history was reached when the Reverends

William Henry Miles and Richard Vanderhorst, on the fifth day of the 1870 General Conference, were elected to serve as bishops of this new denomination. These men were the proud products of the plantation missions, where they had been schooled and prepared for the historic moment when Bishops Paine and McTyeire of the MECS would lay their consecrated hands on the first bishops of the Colored Methodist Episcopal Church. From the shadows of the plantation, a new denomination was born.

One unidentified black preacher expressed the joy he felt when Miles took Bishop Paine's position at the podium: "When I saw that white bishop get out of that chair and a colored bishop take his place, I felt awful—and I feel awful yet—and I wish we may never need a white bishop in that chair again."[78] The awe-inspiring "awful" feeling was an unspeakable joy—a joy and amazement at how forty-one men, five years removed from slavery, had fashioned a fledgling denomination on the anvil of political chicanery and contradictory advice from friends and foes alike.

The majority of the black religious leaders who rose to prominence in these early years had been slave preachers and had emerged from the training provided by plantation missions and other less visible institutions, which had existed simultaneously. They laid the foundation for a church that no subsequent oppression could abolish. These leaders were recognized and respected for their leadership ability by the MECS as well as by the former slave community. Isaac Lane, for example, was known to have gained "the confidence and respect of both white and colored people."[79] The able leadership of those pioneers accounts for the phenomenal success of the newly formed CME when the mantle of leadership was transferred to them and they began evangelizing and organizing conferences.

Bishop William Henry Miles

The first five bishops elected after the Civil War's end ranged in age from twenty-four (Holsey) to fifty-three (Vanderhorst). The other three, Miles, Beebe, and Lane were in their thirties. Each bishop was a former slave, and it was not until 1941 that the CME elected a free-born person as bishop, one who had never experienced human bondage.[80]

Many early black plantation mission preachers achieved literacy, became skilled artisans, purchased freedom, and obtained licenses and even ordination from mainline white churches. William Henry Miles, a light-skinned Kentucky minister and one of the patriarchs of the CME, is a notable example of a pioneer who ascended from slavery to become the first bishop of the CME Church. He was born into slavery on December 26, 1828, in Springfield, Kentucky. Miles was the property of Mary and Edward Miles. He was legally manumitted by the will of his owner, Mary Miles, in 1854, but he remained a houseman until 1864.[81] On December 24, 1849, Miles was married to Francis Ellen Arnold, and his wedding was officiated by a white minister of the MECS. As two of the other early bishops of the CME Church, Miles was a house slave, mulatto, and enjoyed a status superior to field slaves. Dr. Samuel Watson, a white observer at the Organizing General Conference of the CME Church, described Bishop Miles as "bright," but Bishop Vanderhorst said in the General Conference, Miles "is black enough for us."[82] These comments reinforce the conclusion that, since race is such a pervasive issue in America, color consciousness has been a determining factor in nearly every facet of the African-American experience—including religious experience and the recognition of ecclesiastical calling.[83]

On the heels of Miles's conversion, he felt the call to preach. He became affiliated with the MECS in 1855 and was licensed to preach in 1857. Miles was recommended to the Louisville Annual Conference for deacon orders by the Lebanon and Springfield Station Quarterly Conference in 1859.[84] The Whites in the local conference clearly recognized Miles's superior talents, and he was ordained deacon by Bishop Anderson. However, after the war and before the denomination had decided the fate of its black members and ministers, he was told by the presiding elder of the MECS that white members had no place for black members in their church.[85]

After being pushed out of the MECS, Miles joined the AMEZ annual conference and was appointed the pastor of Center Street Church in Louisville, Kentucky, in 1867. Following Miles's short tenure at Center Street Church, Bishop Logan appointed Miles to serve as a traveling missionary to evangelize to and organize churches.[86] After Miles did not receive financial support, he resigned his missionary post. In the meantime, he learned from the Reverend Thomas Taylor of the MECS that the denomination was organizing separate black annual conferences and that when three or more conferences had been formed, a black General Conference would be called to elect bishops and organize what eventually would become the CME Church. This afforded Miles an opportunity to return to his "other church."[87] Upon Miles's return to the MECS, the Reverend Thomas appointed him to organize black conferences and congregations in Kentucky.[88]

Bishop Richard H. Vanderhorst

Richard H. Vanderhorst, the second bishop of the CME, was born in Georgetown, South Carolina, on December 15, 1813. His slave mistresses were Betsy and Judeth Wragg. During his boyhood, he was their body servant. On Sunday, he carried the hymnbooks and Bibles of his mistresses, and there was a special stool designated for him to sit beside them in church. When the worship service ended, he would take their books back home. He became an apprentice under Samuel Dunmore, a black man and exhorter in the MECS, who taught him carpentry. After relocating to Charleston, South Carolina, he joined the Trinity Episcopal Church South, and he became a class leader for the slave members of the church. During those days, Blacks were forbidden licensure to preach by the state and the discipline of southern Methodism. In spite of his limited opportunities to exercise his calling to preach, Vanderhorst heeded the call of the black members of the MECS in 1868 to come to Augusta, Georgia, to help evangelize and organize black conferences and congregations.[89]

Bishop Joseph A. Beebe

Joseph A. Beebe, the third bishop of the CME, was born a slave in Fayetteville, North Carolina, on June 25, 1832. His father and grandfather were gifted preachers.[90] He was one of seventeen children and the fourth in his family to become a preacher. Beebe and his parents were the property of one Melinda Beebe, a devout Methodist who abhorred slavery. She manumitted Beebe's mother Betty, giving the reason that Betty had too many children.[91] When Joseph Beebe, Betty's sixteenth child and seventh son, was born, Melinda went to Betty's cabin and said, "That is going to be a great child."[92] The former slaveholder had read the story in the Bible where Moses was an adopted child and became the leader of his people, which inspired her to adopt Joseph Beebe. She took Beebe under her custody when he was one year old. In an ironic twist on the incident with Pharaoh's daughter, Melinda took Joseph's oldest sister to be his nurse.[93] In defiance of the Anti-Literacy Law, Miss Melinda taught her adopted son to read the Bible. He joined the church at eight years of age and was protected from the rigors of the field servants. Beebe, like most of the early pioneers of colored Methodism, was bivocational. He learned the cobbler's trade, and his adopted mother provided the means to start a business, a successful and popular shoe shop. Beebe's business grew to the extent that he hired nine employees. In addition to his success in business, Beebe served as an effective pastor, presiding elder, and organizer for years. He validated his ministry by serving his people. For example, he paid doctor bills and buried those who were too poor to own sufficient insurance. His home became a foster care facility for twenty-one children, both black and white. His meritorious service earned him the title not only of bishop but also "the beloved leader, the man of divinity, the Christian brother and father."[94] Black preachers historically have addressed the social as well as the spiritual needs of their people—a statement for which Beebe serves as an exemplary model.

Bishop Isaac Lane

Isaac Lane, a pioneer black Methodist in Tennessee, built upon his experiences of the plantation missions during slavery. He was

112

born March 3, 1834, in Madison County, Tennessee, about five miles from Jackson. Lane remembered his white father as a "Methodist of purest type."[95] He also applauded his father for refusing to sell him for substantial profit, and when his wife's master left Tennessee for Arkansas, Isaac's master purchased Isaac's wife and children. Though both Lane and Lucius Holsey were sons of white slave masters, their reflections and assessments of human bondage were quite different. Lane wrote:

> Pen will never be able to record, tongue will never describe the trials, the sufferings and the heartaches of those days. Truly, slavery furnishes the blackest chapter in the history of the American republic and it is the greatest and foulest crime of the nation.[96]

Isaac Lane had no formal educational training. He was the product of a religion without letters, a time when it was against the law to teach Blacks to read and write. Lane lamented the experience: "I learned to read and write under the greatest difficulties. I was not only deprived of a teacher, but I was not allowed to the use of a book or a pencil. I had to learn the best I could."[97] Shortly after his conversion in 1854, Lane attested, "I was overcome with a feeling that I ought to preach."[98] He immediately shared the experience with a man he had admired for his Christian piety. The man directed Lane to his minister for counsel but gave him "no encouragement" because he did not believe in Negroes preaching.[99] This experience reinforced for Lane that race mattered. Lane then turned to a black man for advice. This time, he was reassured, and the man told him that if God had called him to preach he would succeed; the black man exhorted him to trust in God rather than in humanity.

As with other forerunners of the denomination, Lane's ministry was conceived and nurtured in a biracial church milieu, where he worshiped with both Blacks and Whites. Lane petitioned the Quarterly Conference of the MECS for license to preach in 1856, but instead of being licensed to preach, he was granted license to exhort in 1856 and license to preach a decade later in 1866.[100] A white minister, the Reverend A. K. Wilson, became Lane's lifelong friend and "took a lively interest in his career and work."[101] Many of the early black preachers were nurtured by and served an apprenticeship under white ministers. With the growing expectation of freedom and unrest on the eve of the Civil War, however, the southern white denominations became reluctant to license black preachers.

Black leaders, such as Miles, Vanderhorst, Beebe, Lucius H. Holsey, and Lane, placed a high premium on education and training for themselves and their people. The MECS provided Lane, Holsey, Miles, and many others with opportunities for training and the cultivation of their gifts and graces. After Lane was licensed, he was invited to many churches to preach and exhort, especially on Sunday afternoons. Lane attracted large crowds of Blacks and Whites when he preached.

For slave preachers—indeed for these first bishops—the conversion experience was a necessary credential to validate their call to preach. In the antebellum South, slave preachers had to be recommended and endorsed by a white minister to be licensed and receive permission to preach. Since slaves had no formal training, their qualifications for ministry were based on their character and the depth and drama of their conversion experience. Without conversion, the preacher had no testimony. Depending on a burning rather than a learning, the content of slave preachers' exhortations often centered on their conversion experience. After emancipated, many former slaves became literate and outstanding leaders. But the pattern had been set, and their conversion experiences continued to be incorporated into their sermons.

All of the early bishops, without exception, expressed the feeling of needing to be better trained for the ministry.[102] The educational opportunities that the white Southerners offered their former slaves was one reason for the reluctance of Blacks to leave the church of their former masters. In response to the AME's appeal to lure black Methodists away from the MECS, Miles, for example, made it clear that black members of the MECS "were born and raised in the south and expected to be here."[103] The early leaders of the CME were understandably reluctant to severe ties with the MECS because of the opportunities and resources that their former slaveholders promised.[104]

Bishop Henry McNeal Turner

In the 1850s, the Reverend Henry McNeal Turner began a preaching mission in towns and cities in Georgia and South Carolina. In the spring of 1858, in Athens, Georgia, members of the MECS sponsored a weeklong revival. Reverend Turner, who would later become a bishop in the AME Church, was the revivalist. Turner was zealous in his ministry to convert those who had not been saved. Turner's passion to evangelize the unconverted and teach the unlettered to read emanated from his own conversion experience. He had fasted and prayed for God to help him learn to read and write. And despite the laws forbidding Blacks to become literate, Turner believed God would make it possible for him to read and write. Turner reported that he had night visitations from heaven that helped him read Webster's speller and the Bible. He maintained that he would not receive a visit from this dream teacher "unless [he] would study the lessons with [his] greatest effort and kneel down and pray for God's assistance before going to sleep."[105]

Turner was converted between 1848 and 1851. At that time, an older white minister named Jim Weems would take Turner into the woods and pray for his conversion. According to Turner, the impediments that hindered his conversion were the temptations of cursing and drinking whiskey. However, his conversion seemed to have been completed in dramatic fashion while attending a revival at Sharon Camp Ground. After hearing a plantation missionary there, Turner "fell upon the ground, rolled in the dirt, foamed at the mouth and agonized under conviction until Christ relieved him by [Christ's] atoning blood."[106]

Bishop Lucius H. Holsey

It was under the powerful preaching of Turner that a young Holsey "experienced a change of heart and became a zealous member of the church."[107] Holsey was a product of pietistic and evangelical Christianity in which converts "got religion."[108] However, Holsey—as Holsey tells it—wanted to get as much mileage as possible from his conversion experience, so he waited to officially join the church until the last day of the revival when a white evangelist, the Reverend W. A. Parks, preached the Sunday sermon. Parks noticed that a sixteen-year-old slave remained at the altar after most of the congregation had departed. Noticing that the young man had remained behind, Parks announced to those leaving, "Brethren, I believe God will convert this boy right now. Let us gather around him and pray for him."[109] After Holsey's conversion was validated by the white preacher, he confessed that the "Lord rolled the burden of sin from my heart and heaven's light came shining in. Oh, what a happy boy I was!"[110] With tears streaming down his cheeks, Holsey looked into the face of the minister, pointed his forefinger upward and said, "Brother, when you get to Heaven and the Blessed Lord places a crown on your head, I will be one star in that crown."[111]

Holsey was a product of his environment and times. In comparison to many other servants in bondage, the peculiar institution had been kind to Holsey. He was a house servant, which afforded him some privileges denied the field laborers. In his assessment of slavery, he echoed the sentiment Phillis Wheatley had expressed almost a century earlier:

> I have no complaint against American slavery. It was a blessing in disguise to me and to many. It has made the negro race what it could not have been in its native land. Slavery was but a circumstance or a link in the transitions of humanity, and must have its greatest bearing upon the future.[112]

Holsey was not alone in his paternalistic "blessing-in-disguise" attitude about the enslavement of Africans. Other slaves, including the more radical Bishop Turner of the AME Church and George L. Knox, editor of the *Indianapolis Freeman,* accepted slavery as a training ground for civilization and Christianization. Even Booker T. Washington viewed slavery as a "divine plan for black progress."[113]

Holsey "represent[ed] a faithful product of the mission zeal," and "his fidelity to trust and zeal caused him to be appointed a local preacher before emancipation."[114] The MECS often identified the slaves with unusual talents and leadership potential and intentionally cultivated paternalistic relationships with them. Bishop George F. Pierce, the son of Dr. Lovick Pierce, a leader in the MECS, for example, tutored Holsey in theology. There was a genuine loyalty and bonding in their master-slave relationship. In 1862, Holsey married Harriet Anne Turner, the personal servant of George Pierce's daughter. Both Holsey and Harriet were house servants of Pierce, who officiated at their wedding held in his home.[115]

In his autobiography, Holsey called Sparta, Georgia, the birthplace of colored Methodism and the place where his religious formation was under the direction of Bishop Pierce.[116] In 1866, Holsey worked ardently to secure the first lot and to oversee the construction of the first church parsonage for the Georgia Colored Conference, as mandated by the 1866 General Conference of the MECS. Throughout 1867, he traveled the state to organize old slave preachers of the MECS. He lobbied to get them to bring into existence black Methodism.[117]

The Sparta congregation was considered the "colored elite."[118] Many of the members were mulattoes as their pastor Holsey. It is apparent that intraracial conflicts and jealousies were often orchestrated by the white establishment in order to control Blacks in the South. There frequently was tension between the light-skinned and dark-skinned African Americans. A member of Holsey's own congregation observed that racial attitudes in the black community represented "three hundred years of degradation . . . and they deeply believed . . . that people with white skins [were] superior to people with black skins."[119] Holsey himself in fact may have believed the idea of the "inferiority" of the African culture, owing to his own lack of education about the richness of African heritage and history.[120]

The following episode, told by Adele Logan Alexander, is significant:

[One Sunday morning] when a heavyset, dark-skinned woman wearing a bandanna around her head, an apron, and generally shabby clothing supposedly rushed into the service at the Ebenezer church and positioned herself in a front-row pew, interrupting Bishop Holsey's sermon. Her color, her unpolished manner, and her dress immediately told the more affluent and lighter-skinned parishioners, decked out in their finest attire, that she was neither a member nor an invited guest. The woman fanned herself, gasped for breath, and tried to recover from her exertions while the minister and church members stared in stunned silence following her unexpected intrusion. Then, slowly, a solemn hymn reportedly swelled around the visitor as the congregation began to sing:

> None but the yellow,
> None but the yellow,
> None but the yellow . . . shall see God.[121]

Thus ends the account of an eyewitness family member of Adele Logan Alexander, a member of Ebenezer CME Church, Sparta, Georgia.

CONCLUSION

This horrific tale of "witness" is a fitting summary to a book entitled *Hell Without Fire*. After four hundred years of enslavement—an institution that encouraged African Americans to hate everything about themselves, and that in the name of "conversion"—African Americans had been told that they had no history worth remembering, no ancestors worth honoring, no family worth supporting, and no religion worth practicing. African Americans even on the verge of freedom consequently were less than sure of their identity. They had embraced conflicting stories about African religion, history, and culture. One of the greatest crimes American slavery committed against Blacks was its instruction in hating themselves and their own people.

In spite of the dehumanizing residues of slavery, many newly freed African Americans felt a greater bond to their local communities and religion than they did to their northern liberators or their African heritage. They realized that freedom without employment, shelter, food, and clothing continued to make their existence a precarious one. Consequently, their first allegiances were to maintain their southern relationships and associations in order to build their own schools and independent denomination—to secure their future and to rise unconsumed from the pyre of their past.

NOTES

Introduction

1. Jon Butler, *Awash in a Sea of Faith: Christianizing the American People* (Cambridge, Mass.: Harvard University Press, 1990), 157.

2. James Albert Ukawsaw Gronniosaw, *A Narrative of the Most Remarkable Particulars in the Life of James Albert Ukawsaw Gronniosaw, An African Prince* (Glascow: David Robertson, Tronsgate, 1840), iii.

3. Ibid., 208-9.

4. Ibid., vii.

5. Jonathan Edwards, "Sinners in the Hands of an Angry God" in *Selected Writings of Jonathan Edwards,* ed. Harold P. Simonson (New York: Frederick Ungar Publishing, 1970), 104, 107.

6. James Melvin Washington, *Conversations with God: Two Centuries of Prayers by African Americans* (New York: HarperCollins, 1994), 51.

7. Mechal Sobel, *The World They Made Together: Black and White Values in Eighteenth-Century Virginia* (Princeton, N.J.: Princeton University Press, 1987), 201.

8. Ibid.

9. Ibid., 199.

10. Ibid., 201.

11. Ibid., 200.

12. Originally quoted in William Ferris, "The Negro Conversion," *Keystone Folklore Quarterly* 15 (Spring 1970): 49. Later quoted in Yolanda Pierce, "How Saul Became Paul: The African-American Conversion Experience," *Griot* 19, 2 (2000): 3.

13. Sobel, *The World They Made Together,* 3.

14. Peter H. Wood, "Jesus Christ Has Got Thee at Last," *The Bulletin of the Center for the Study of Southern Culture and Religion* 3, 3 (November 1979): 1.

15. Ibid.

16. Samuel Davies, *Letters from the Reverend Samuel Davies, and Others; Shewing the State of Religion in Virginia, South Carolina, and Particularly among the Negroes,* 2nd ed. (London: J. & W. Oliver, 1757).

17. George Whitefield, *The Works of the Reverend George Whitefield,* 6 vols. (London, 1771–1772), 4:35-41.

Chapter 1: Context for Conversion

1. Danicl P. Mannix, *Black Cargoes: A History of the Atlantic Slave Trade: 1518–1833* (New York: Viking Press, 1962), 10.

2. Bartholomew de las Casas, a Catholic priest, allegedly initiated the idea of enslaving Africans and sending them to the New World. He rationalized his plans on the humanitarian ground of using Africans to protect Native Americans from human bondage. See Arthur Helps, *The Life of Las Casas: The Apostle of the Indies* (London: George Bell and Sons, 1896), 67.

3. Mannix, *Black Cargoes*, 2-3.

4. Ibid., 4.

5. On October 18, 1564, a slave fleet of four vessels, consisting of the *Jesus,* 700 tons; *the Solomon,* 140 tons; the bark *Tiger,* 50 tons; and the pinnace *Swallow,* 30 tons, set sail from Teneriffe to Senor de Ponte. The ship *Jesus* was the guardian vessel that the other smaller ships were ordered to take to for direction and protection. See George Francis Dow, *Slave Ships and Slaving* (Port Washington, N.Y.: Kennikat Press, 1969), 22. This is an excellent source for providing the names of the slave ships.

6. Gomes Eannes De Azurara, *The Chronicle of Discovery and Conquest of Guinea,* vol. 1, trans. Charles R. Beazley and Edgar Prestage (London: Hakluyt Society, 1896–1899), 50-51. Albert J. Raboteau, *Slave Religion: The "Invisible Institution" in the Antebellum South* (New York: Oxford University Press, 1978), 96.

7. Carter G. Woodson, *The Education of the Negro Prior to 1861: A History of the Education of the Colored People of the United States from the Beginning of Slavery to the Civil War* (New York: G. P. Putnam's Sons, 1915), 18-19.

8. Raboteau, *Slave Religion,* 96.

9. A. F. C. Ryder, *Benin and the Europeans: 1485–1897* (New York: Humanities Press, 1969), 32.

10. Ibid.

11. Ibid., 47.

12. Ibid.

13. John Thornton, *Africa and Africans in the Making of the Atlantic World, 1400–1800,* 2nd ed. (Cambridge: Cambridge University Press, 1998), 98-99.

14. Ibid., 9

15. Ibid.

16. Folarin Shyllon, *Black People in Britain: 1555–1833* (London: Oxford University Press, 1977), 6.

17. Mannix, *Black Cargoes,* vii.

18. Ibid., 11.

19. John Hope Franklin, *From Slavery to Freedom: The History of the Negro* (New York: Alfred A. Knopf, 1980), 41-49.

20. Mary Frances Berry and John W. Blassingame, *Long Memory: The Black Experience in America* (New York: Oxford University Press, 1982), 6.

21. Ibid., 5.

22. Ibid., 4-7.

23. Ibid., 4.

24. Ibid., 7.

25. Ibid., 7-9.

26. Mannix, *Black Cargoes,* ix.

27. Winthrop D. Jordan, *The White Man's Burden: Historical Origin of Racism in the United States* (New York: Oxford University Press, 1974), 4. There is no consensus among scholars as to the genesis of racism in America. There are those who would contend that racial prejudice emanated from slavery. However, historians such as Earl N. Degler argue that racism preceded and preconditioned slavery. From my observations and research, I tend to support Winthrop D. Jordan who maintains that the enslavement of Africans and white antipathy toward them appear simulta-

neously. Therefore, prejudice and slavery were generated from each other. However, the rudiments for racism were in place when the early European settlers arrived in the New World.

28. Frank M. Snowden Jr., *Blacks in Antiquity: Ethiopians in the Greco-Roman Experience* (Cambridge, Mass.: Belknap Press, 1970), 174-75.

29. Ibid., 180.

30. Raboteau, *Slave Religion*, 152.

31. Archives of Maryland, I: Proceedings and Acts of the General Assembly of Maryland, January 1637–September 1664 (Baltimore: Maryland Historical Society, 1883), 526-27.

32. Ibid.

33. Wilborn Waller Hening, *Statutes at Large; Being a Collection of All the Laws of Virginia, from the First Session of the Legislature in the Year 1619*, vol. 2 (New York: R. & W. & G. Bartow, 1823), 260.

34. Archives of Maryland, I, 526-33.

35. Fundamental Constitution, 1669–1670, in North Carolina Colonial Records, I, 204, and Revision of 1698, D. J. McCord, Statues of South Carolina, III, 343 (Act of 1690) and 364-65 (not of 1712). Colonial Laws of New York, I (1706), 597-98. The New Jersey Act was passed in 1704 but was disallowed (N. Trutt, Laws of the British Plantations in America), 257; Acts of Privy Council, Colonial Series, 1680–1720, 848.

36. H. P. Thompson, *Into All Lands: History of the Society for the Propagation of the Gospel in Foreign Parts: 1701–1950* (London: SPCK, 1951), 44-45. According to Arthur Helps, las Casas was told by the colonists that if license was given to them to import a dozen Negro slaves each, they would set the Indians free. Helps quotes las Casas as saying that his suggestion "to bring Negro slaves to these lands . . . not considering the injustice with which the Portuguese take them, and make them slaves; which advice . . . he would not have given for all he had in the world" (see Helps, *Life of las Casas*, 67. Also see Carter G. Woodson, *The History of the Negro Church* [Washington, D.C.: Associated Publishers, 1921]).

37. Kenneth N. Stampp, *The Peculiar Institution: Slavery in the Ante-Bellum South* (New York: Vintage Books, 1955), 23.

38. Jon Butler, *Awash in a Sea of Faith: Christianizing the American People* (Cambridge, Mass.: Harvard University Press, 1990), 158-59.

39. Stanley M. Elkins, *Slavery: A Problem in American Institutional and Intellectual Life*, 2nd ed. (Chicago: University of Chicago Press, 1969), 103-15.

40. Richard Hofstadter, *America at 1750: A Social Portrait* (New York: Alfred A. Knopf, 1971), 90.

41. E. Franklin Frazier, *The Negro Family in the United States* (Chicago: University of Chicago Press, 1939), 21.

42. L. Henry Whelchel Jr., "'My Chains Fell Off': Heart Religion in the African American Methodist Tradition," in *"Heart Religion" in the Methodist Tradition and Related Movements*, ed. Richard B. Steele (Lanham, Md.: Scarecrow Press, 2001), 97-98.

43. John Michael Vlach, *The Afro-American Tradition in Decorative Art* (Cleveland: Cleveland Museum of Art, 1978), 36.

44. Harry V. Richardson, *The Negro in American Religious Life*, The Negro Heritage Library, vol.1 (1966), 381.

45. Justo L. González, *The Story of Christianity* (San Francisco: Harper & Row, 1985), 205.

46. Ibid., 207.

47. Melville J. Herskovits, *The Myth of the Negro Past* (Boston: Beacon Press, 1990), 208.

48. Ibid., 210.

49. *The Works of the Reverend John Wesley,* vol. 2 (New York: J. Emory and B. Waught, 1831), 433. William B. McClain called Wesley's first African converts "the nameless two." See William B. McClain, *Black People in the Methodist Church* (Cambridge, Mass.: Schenkman Publishing, 1984), 7.

50. Grant S. Shockley, ed., *Heritage and Hope: The African-American Presence in United Methodism* (Nashville: Abingdon Press, 1991), 27-28. Lars P. Qualben, *A History of the Christian Church* (New York: Thomas Nelson, 1942), 541.

51. Raboteau, *Slave Religion,* 152. The Second Great Awakening, in New England in particular, ushered in reform and radical moral transformation. The evangelists stressed a radical amendment to behavior as a necessary and concomitant sign of true conversion. The fervor from the revivals created the climate to produce Harriet Beecher Stowe's *Uncle Tom's Cabin,* which had a pervasive impact on slavery. See Sydney E. Ahlstrom, *A Religious History of the American People* (New Haven, Conn.: Yale University Press, 1972), 415-28.

52. Thornton, *Africa and Africans,* 270.

53. Ibid., 235-36.

54. James Albert Ukawsaw Gronniosaw, *A Narrative of the Most Remarkable Particulars in the Life of James Albert Ukawsaw Gronniosaw, An African Prince* (Glascow: David Robertson, Tronsgate, 1840), 23.

55. Robin Horton, "African Conversion," *Africa* 41 (April 1971): 94.

56. Samuel Davies, *Letters from the Reverend Samuel Davies, and Others; Shewing the State of Religion in Virginia, South Carolina, and Particularly among the Negroes,* 2nd ed. (London, J. & W. Oliver, 1757), 30.

57. Samuel Davies, *The State of Religion among the Protestant Dissenters in Virginia* (Boston: S. Kneeland, 1751), 23.

58. Ibid.

59. Raboteau, *Slave Religion,* 306.

60. Ibid.

61. C. Eric Lincoln and Lawrence H. Mamiya, "The Religious Dimension: 'The Black Sacred Cosmos,'" in *Down by the Riverside: Reading in African American Religion,* ed. Larry G. Murphy (New York: New York University Press, 2000), 34.

62. Gronniosaw, *Narrative of the Most Remarkable Particulars,* 53.

63. Ibid.

64. Sylvia R. Frey and Betty Wood, *Come Shouting to Zion: African American Protestantism in the American South and British Caribbean* (Chapel Hill: University of North Carolina Press, 1998), 84.

65. Ibid.

66. Peter H. Wood, "Jesus Christ Has Got Thee at Last," *The Bulletin of the Center for the Study of Southern Culture and Religion* 3, 3 (November 1979): 6. Also recorded in Jeffrey J. Crow, *The Black Experience in Revolutionary North Carolina* (Raleigh, N.C.: Department of Cultural Resources, 1977), 47.

67. Ibid.

68. *Virginia Gazette*

69. Ellen Gibson Wilson, *The Loyal Blacks* (New York: Capricorn Books, 1976), 13.

70. Dena J. Epstein, *Sinful Tunes and Spirituals: Black Folk Music to the Civil War* (Urbana: University of Illinois Press, 1977), 109; from Beilby Porteus, "An Essay Towards a Plan for the More Effectual Civilization and Conversion of the Negro Slave," *Tracts on Various Subjects* (London: L. Hansard and Sons, 1807), 174-75, 182-87.

Chapter 2: Conversion and Religious Training

1. George Keith, *An Exhortation and Caution to Friends Concerning Buying or Keeping of Negroes* (Philadelphia: n.p., 1889), 5; this is one of the earliest printed protests against slavery in America.

2. Henry W. Haynes, "Cotton Mather and His Slaves," *Proceeding of the American Antiquarian Society, New Series,* vol. 11 (Worchester: American Antiquarian Society, 1889), 194. Cotton Mather's essay *The Negro Christianized* (Boston: B. Green, 1706) is a rare book in the Boston Public Library.

3. Carter G. Woodson, *The Education of the Negro Prior to 1861* (New York: G. P. Putnam's Sons, 1915), 18.

4. Ibid., 19-20

5. Ibid., 20.

6. Ibid., 22.

7. Ibid.

8. The Code Noir obliged every planter to have his Negroes instructed and baptized. It allowed for the slaves' instruction, worship, and rest not only every Sunday, but also every festival usually observed by the Roman Catholic Church. It did not permit any market to be held on Sundays or holidays. It prohibited, under severe penalties, all masters and managers from corrupting their female slaves. It did not allow the Negro husband, wife, or infant children to be sold separately. It forbade the use of torture or immoderate and inhuman punishments. It obliged the owners to maintain their old and decrepit slaves. If the Negroes were not fed and clothed as the law prescribed, or if they were in any way cruelly treated, they might apply to the procurer, who was obliged by his office to protect them (Woodson, *Education of the Negro,* 23).

9. Ibid., 28-29.

10. The Reverend Charles Martyn said, "They become lazy and proud, entertaining high opinion of themselves and neglecting their daily labor" (See Charles Martyn to Philip Bearcroft, St. Andrews, South Carolina, June 25, 1952, in S.P.G. MSS [L.C. Trans.] 1, B20, No. 137).

11. Frank J. Klingberg, *An Appraisal of the Negro in Colonial South Carolina* (Philadelphia: Porcupine Press, 1975), 8.

12. Ibid, 9.

13. Robert Stevens to the Society for the Propagation of the Gospel (n. d.) Goose Creek, S.C., in S.P.G. MSS (L.C. Trans.) A2, No. 1.

14. Klingberg, *Appraisal of the Negro,* 9.

15. Ibid., 14.

16. Ibid., 16.

17. Ibid., 26.

18. Ibid., 18.

19. "Inanimate things take on far greater importance and are endowed with emotions, intentions. The moon rules the tides, and the tides rule birth and death. . . . Rivers drown experienced fishermen who catch too many fish in their waters; cotton gins cut off fingers and arms of people who make them work when they are weary; lightning strikes proudful trees that strive to outdo their fellows and stretch their heads up into the sky" (Julia Peterkin, *Roll, Jordan, Roll* [New York: R. O. Ballou, 1933], 146; reprinted in Klingberg, *Appraisal of the Negro,* 20).

20. Klingberg, *Appraisal of the Negro,* 45-46.

21. Ibid., 45.

22. "Negro Preachers Serving Whites," in *Negro History Bulletin* 3 (October 1939): 8, 15.

23. Woodson, *Education of the Negro,* 29.

24. Ibid., 34.

25. Ibid., 35.

26. Ibid., 10.

27. Ibid.

28. Ibid. Cotton Mather also advocated teaching the children in the slave families to read so that they may teach others to read the catechism (see *The Negro Christianized*, 28). It is interesting to note that black children and youth historically have been major contributors to the freedom of African Americans. In the seventeenth century, the Society for the Propagation of the Gospel used African children to teach adults how to read and write. In the twentieth century, the Southern Christian Leadership Conference enlisted children to save the civil rights movement from a devastating defeat. During the 1963 Birmingham civil rights movement, one of the leaders commented, "We needed more troops. We had scraped the bottom of the barrel of adults who would go [to jail]." The decision to involve the children in the demonstrations redeemed the 1960s civil rights movement in Birmingham from defeat. See Stephen B. Oates, *Let the Trumpet Sound: The Life of Martin Luther King, Jr.* (New York: Harper & Row, 1982), 232.

29. George Whitefield, *A Journal of a Voyage from London to Savannah in Georgia* in *George Whitefield's Journals* (London: Banner of Truth Trust, 1960), 445-46.

30. John Wesley admonished slave masters for their inhumane treatment of slaves and lack of concern for their religious training. He cited Hugh Bryan as a paragon for slaveholders. See John Wesley, *Thoughts upon Heaven* (London: R. Hawes, 1774), 6-7.

31. The Reverend George Whitefield and the Bryans were noted for their success in bringing religion to the Negroes on the Bryan plantation. Some of their servants established the first churches in Savannah. And the Bryans organized a school for Blacks on their plantation in Prince William Parish (Gerhard Spieler, "Lowcountry Settler Helped Area Slaves," *The Beaufort Gazette*, 28 July 1991, sec. C, p. 7).

32. "The first Negro Baptist Church in America, according to Dr. W. H. Brooks, was founded by one Mr. Palmer at Silver Bluff [South Carolina] across the river from Augusta, Georgia, in the colony of South Carolina, some time between the years 1773 and 1775." George Galphin was a kind slave master who permitted George Liele to exhort among his slaves. George Liele was born in Virginia around 1750. He later moved to Burke County, Georgia, with his master, Henry Sharpe. Liele attended his master's church and was converted and baptized. His ministerial gifts and graces, not usually found in converted slaves, surfaced, and Liele was permitted to preach to plantation slaves living along the Savannah River (Carter G. Woodson, *The History of the Negro Church* [Washington, D.C.: Associated Publishers, 1921], 41-44).

33. Ibid., 48-49.

34. Ibid., 49.

35. "Letter showing the Rise and Progress of Early Negro Churches of Georgia and West Indies," *The Journal of Southern History* 53 (August 1987): 77.

36. Ibid., 79.

37. Ibid.

38. Ibid., 83.

39. *Boston Weekly News-Letter* (21 August 1740).

40. Frank Lambert, "'I Saw the Book Talk': Slave Readings of the First Great Awakening," *The Journal of Negro History* 77 (Fall 1992): 187; also see *Boston Weekly News-Letter* (21 August 1740).

41. Samuel Davies, *The Duty of Christians to Support Missionaries to the Heathens* (Boston: n.p., 1830), 34; also see Winthrop D. Jordan, *White Over Black*:

American Attitudes Toward the Negro, 1550–1812 (Chapel Hill: University of North Carolina Press, 1968), 188.

42. Samuel Davies, *Letters from the Reverend Samuel Davies, and Others; Shewing the State of Religion in Virginia, South Carolina, and Particularly among the Negroes,* 2nd ed. (London: J. & W. Oliver, 1757), 15.

43. Sylvia R. Frey and Betty Wood, *Come Shouting to Zion: African American Protestantism in the American South and British Caribbean to 1830* (Chapel Hill: University of North Carolina Press, 1998), 85.

44. Ibid.

45. Ibid.

46. Lambert, "I Saw the Book Talk," 191.

47. James B. Lawrence, "Religious Education of the Negro in the Colony of Georgia," *Georgia Historical Quarterly* 19 (March 1930): 4.

48. Ibid.

49. James Albert Ukawsaw Gronniosaw, *A Narrative of the Most Remarkable Particulars in the Life of James Albert Ukawsaw Gronniosaw, An African Prince* (Glascow: David Robertson, Tronsgate, 1840), 10-11.

50. William S. White, *The African Preacher: An Authentic Narrative* (Freeport, N.Y.: Books for Libraries Press, 1972), 11-12. Lambert, "I Saw the Book Talk," 187-88.

51. Charles A. Raymond, "The Religious Life of the Negro Slave," *Harper's New Monthly Magazine* 27 (1863): 482.

52. Ibid., 482-83. Also see Eugene D. Genovese, *Roll, Jordan, Roll: The World the Slaves Made* (New York: Pantheon Books, 1974), 266-67.

53. Raymond, "The Religious Life of the Negro Slave," 482.

54. Ibid., 477; also see Klingberg, *An Appraisal of the Negro,* 16.

55. Milton C. Sernett, *Afro-American Religious History: A Documentary Witness* (Durham, N.C.: Duke University Press, 1985), 27.

56. See the article, "Negro Preachers Serving Whites," *The Negro History Bulletin* (October 1939): 8.

57. Charles V. Hamilton, *The Black Preacher in America* (New York: William Morrow & Co., 1972), 42-43.

58. Ibid.

59. W. E. B. DuBois, *Souls of Black Folks: Essays and Sketches* (New York: Blue Heron Press, 1953), 211.

60. Genovese, *Roll, Jordan, Roll,* 256.

61. Ibid., 266.

62. Joseph A. Johnson Jr., *The Soul of the Black Preacher* (Philadelphia: Pilgrim Press, 1971), 11-12.

63. Joseph E. Holloway, ed., *Africanisms in American Culture* (Bloomington, Ind.: Indiana University Press, 1990), 108.

64. Carter G. Woodson, *The Mis-education of the Negro* (Trenton, N.J.: Africa World Press, 1990), 52.

65. Dorothy Porter, *Early Negro Writings, 1760–1837* (Boston: Beacon Press, 1971), 536.

66. Albert J. Raboteau, *Slave Religion: The "Invisible Institution" in the Antebellum South* (New York: Oxford University Press, 1978), 43.

67. Klingberg, *An Appraisal of the Negro,* 5.

Chapter 3: Conversion and the Plantation Missions

1. Susan Markey Fickling, *Slave Conversion in South Carolina, 1830–1860* (Columbia: University of South Carolina, 1924), 15.

2. Ibid., 15-16.

3. Luther P. Jackson, "Religious Development of the Negro in Virginia from 1760 to 1860," *Journal of Negro History* 16 (April 1931): 217-18.

4. David Walker, *Appeal, in Four Articles; Together with a Preamble, to the Coloured Citizens of the World, but in Particular, and Very Expressly, to Those of the United States of America,* ed. Charles M. Wiltse (New York: Hill and Wang, 1995). Walker's *Appeal* was first published in 1829 and is an African-centered speech attacking white injustice and advocating black self-reliance. Walker was born on September 28, 1785, in Wilmington, North Carolina. His father was a slave, and his mother was free. According to North Carolina law, children inherited the status of the mother, so Walker was born free. He readily established himself in the abolitionist community as a lecturer.

5. Rayford W. Logan and Michael R. Winston, ed., *Dictionary of American Negro Biography* (New York: W. W. Norton and Co., 1982), 623.

6. Carter G. Woodson, *The Education of the Negro Prior to 1861* (New York: G. P. Putnam's Sons, 1915), 179-204.

7. William George Hawkins, *Lunsford Lane* (Boston: Crosby & Nichols, 1863), 65; Mason Crum, *Gullah: Negro Life in the Carolina Sea Islands* (New York: Negro Universities Press, 1968), 202.

8. William Wells Brown, *Narrative of William Wells Brown, A Fugitive Slave* (Boston: The Anti-Slavery Office, 1847), 82-83.

9. Winthrop S. Hudson and John Corrigan, *Religion in America: An Historical Account of the Development of American Religious Life* (Upper Saddle River, N.Y.: Prentice Hall, 1998), 154; also see Donald G. Mathews, *Religion in the Old South* (Chicago: University of Chicago Press, 1977), 102-9.

10. Winthrop S. Hudson, *Religion in America*, 3rd ed. (New York: Charles Scribner's Sons, 1981), 144.

11. Mathews, *Religion in the Old South*, 103-9.

12. Gilbert H. Barnes and Dwight L. Dumond, eds., *Letters of Theodore Dwight Weld* (Gloucester, Mass.: Peter Smith, 1965), 243.

13. *Third Annual Report*, Liberty County Association, 23.

14. Albert J. Raboteau, *Slave Religion: The "Invisible Institution" in the Antebellum South* (New York: Oxford University Press, 1978), 164.

15. Proceedings of the Meeting in Charleston, S.C., May 13-15, 1845, on the religious instruction of the Negroes (Charleston, S.C.: B. Jenkins, 1845), 34-35.

16. Fickling, *Slave Conversion in South Carolina*, 13.

17. Ibid., 14.

18. Charles C. Jones, *The Religious Instruction of the Negroes in the United States,* reprinted ed. (New York: Kraus Reprint Co., 1969), 250-51.

19. Ibid., 252. Some white ministers lamented that in preaching to Negroes, they could not keep the interest of black people and could not make them understand. In response, Jones said, "But it is the duty of ministers to attain to a thorough understanding of the doctrines and duties of Christianity, and to cultivate such a facility of expression and language . . . to unfold both doctrines and duties intelligibly to the weakest hearer" (253).

20. Crum, *Gullah*, 203.

21. Ibid., 226-27.

22. Ibid., 230.

23. *Christian Advocate and Journal* 8 (7 February 1834): 94. Quoted in Crum, *Gullah*, 203.

24. Ibid., 200-202, 230.

25. *Christian Advocate and Journal* 9 (26 June 1835): 174.

26. Jones, *Religious Instruction of the Negroes*, 249.

27. Proceedings of the Meeting in Charleston, S.C., May 13-15, 1845, 48-49.

28. Ibid.

29. Raboteau, *Slave Religion,* 177.

30. David Benedict, *A General History of the Baptist Denomination in America,* vol. 2 (Boston: Lincoln & Edmands, 1813), 190-92; Jones, *Religious Instruction of the Negroes,* 157-58. The Reverend Andrew Bryan of Savannah is the persecuted black preacher to whom reference is made. See also *The New York Times* (8 July 1856), 4.

31. Crum, *Gullah,* 184.

32. Jones, *Religious Instruction of the Negroes,* 255.

33. Fickling, *Slave Conversion in South Carolina,* 17.

34. *Christian Advocate and Journal* 8 (7 February 1834): 9.

35. Col. 4:1, quoted in Crum, *Gullah,* 204.

36. Col. 3:22, quoted in Crum, *Gullah,* 204.

37. Crum, *Gullah,* 204-5.

38. Ibid., 205.

39. Ibid., 198.

40. H. A. Tupper, "History of the First Baptist Church in South Carolina," *Journal of Episcopal Church* (1830): 244; quoted in Fickling, *Slave Conversion in South Carolina,* 22.

41. Fickling, *Slave Conversion in South Carolina,* 22-23.

42. Ibid., 23.

43. Kenneth K. Bailey, "Protestantism and Afro-Americans in the Old South: Another Look," *Journal of Southern History* 41, 4 (November 1975): 463.

44. Ibid., 458.

45. Ibid.

46. Sunbury (Ga.) Baptist Association, *Minutes,* 1832 (Savannah, 1833), 6-7; *Minutes,* 1833 (Savannah, 1833), 6; Emanuel K. Love, *History of the First African Baptist Church, from its Organization, January 20th, 1788, to July 1st, 1888* (Savannah, Morning News Print, 1888), 21-22. Bailey, "Protestantism and Afro-Americans in the Old South," 467.

47. Love, *History of the First African Baptist Church,* 24.

48. Bailey, "Protestantism and Afro-Americans in the Old South," 467.

49. Ibid., 468.

50. Ibid., 469.

51. Ibid.

52. Ibid.

53. Ibid., 140; George Lewis, *Impressions of America and the American Churches* (Edinburgh: W. P. Kennedy, 1845), 129-31.

54. Bailey, "Protestantism and Afro-Americans in the Old South," 470.

55. Raboteau, *Slave Religion,* 179.

Chapter 4: Conversion and the Formation of the Colored Methodist Episcopal Church

1. For further study of the AME Church, see: Richard Allen, *The Life Experience and Gospel Labors of the Rt. Reverend Richard Allen* (Nashville: Abingdon Press, 1983); Carol V. R. George, *Segregated Sabbaths: Richard Allen and the Emergence of Independent Black Churches, 1760–1840* (New York: Oxford University Press, 1973); George A. Singleton, *The Romance of African Methodism: A Study of the*

African Methodist Episcopal Church (New York: Exposition Press, 1952); and Augusta H. Hall Jr., *A Solid Foundation: African Methodism in Georgia* (Lithonia, Ga.: AHH Education System, 2000).

2. For further study of the AMEZ Church, see: David H. Bradley, *A History of the A.M.E. Zion Church* (Nashville: Parthenon Press, 1970); William J. Walls, *The African Methodist Episcopal Zion Church; Reality of the Black Church* (Charlotte, N.C.: A.M.E. Zion Publishing House, 1974).

3. *Journal of the General Conference of the Methodist Episcopal Church,* vol. 2, 1844 (New York: Carlton & Phillips, 1855), 148-49.

4. Walter L. Fleming, ed., *Documentary History of Reconstruction* (New York: McGraw-Hill Book Co., 1966), 2:252.

5. Ibid., 253-54.

6. Ibid.

7. Ibid., 255.

8. Emory Stevens Bucke, ed., *The History of American Methodism,* 3 vols. (New York: Abingdon Press, 1964), 2:65-85.

9. *Journal of the General Conference of the Methodist Episcopal Church, South, 1866,* ed. T. O. Summers (Nashville: A. H. Redford, 1866), 18.

10. Ibid.

11. Ibid.

12. Ibid.

13. Ralph E. Morrow, *Northern Methodism and Reconstruction* (East Lansing: Michigan State University Press, 1956), 130.

14. Hunter Dickinson Farish, *The Circuit Rider Dismounts: A Social History of Southern Methodism, 1865–1900* (Richmond, Va.: Dietz Press, 1938), 136-37.

15. *Christian Recorder* (26 May 1866).

16. Ibid.

17. *Southern Christian Advocate* (1 June 1866).

18. Farish, *Circuit Rider Dismounts,* 135.

19. Ibid.

20. Testimony from Report of the Joint Committee on Reconstruction, 1866, Parts II, III, and IV.

21. L. H. Holsey, *Autobiography, Sermons, Addresses, and Essays* (Atlanta: Franklin Printing and Publishing, 1898), 33.

22. William B. Gravely, "The Social, Political and Religious Significance of the Formation of the Colored Methodist Episcopal Church: 1870," *Methodist History* 18 (October 1979): 13.

23. *Southern Christian Advocate* (1 June 1866).

24. *Southern Christian Advocate* (22 June 1866).

25. Ibid.

26. T. G. Steward, *Fifty Years in the Gospel Ministry* (Philadelphia: AME Book Concern, 1930), 116.

27. Donald G. Mathews, *Religion in the Old South* (Chicago: University of Chicago Press, 1977), 144.

28. *Minutes of the Annual Conferences of the Methodist Episcopal Church, South, for the Year 1866* (Nashville: Southern Methodist Publishing House, 1870), 143.

29. *Christian Recorder* (8 August 1870).

30. Ibid.

31. *Southern Christian Advocate* (8 March 1869).

32. *Christian Recorder* (8 March 1869).

33. "Letter from Kentucky," *Christian Recorder* (18 December 1869).

34. *Christian Recorder* (16 July 1869).

35. Ibid.
36. Ibid.
37. Steward, *Fifty Years in the Gospel Ministry,* 92.
38. Ibid.
39. *Christian Recorder* (5 October 1867).
40. *Christian Advocate* (20 January 1866).
41. *Christian Recorder* (5 October 1867).
42. Ibid.
43. Ibid.
44. Steward, *Fifty Years in the Gospel Ministry,* 116.
45. Ibid.
46. Ibid.
47. *Southern Christian Advocate* (29 January 1869).
48. Jennifer Judith Wojcikowski, "Negotiating Ecclesiastical Identity: Black Southern Methodists and the Creation of the Colored Methodist Episcopal Church in America, 1866–1870" (master's thesis, University of North Carolina at Chapel Hill, 1994), 47.
49. Ibid.
50. Ibid.
51. Holsey, *Autobiography,* 22-23.
52. *Southern Christian Advocate* (15 January 1869).
53. *Southern Christian Advocate* (29 January 1867).
54. C. Eric Lincoln and Lawrence H. Mamiya, *The Black Church in the African American Experience* (Durham, N.C.: Duke University Press, 1990), 130.
55. From the documents reviewed above, it is clear that the years 1866 to 1869 saw black Methodists throughout the South organize themselves into separate ecclesiastical groups. Additional evidence for this activity may be found in a revealing footnote to the 1867 Annual Conference Minutes, which states that "the Bishop and cabinet began organization of a conference for the colored people" (*Minutes of 1867 North Georgia Annual Conference held at Atlanta, Georgia, November 27-December 2,* Bishop George F. Pierce, Presiding Bishop, p. 6). The archives at Pitts Library, Emory University, has a collection of the Methodist Episcopal Church South's Annual Conference Minutes for the North and South Georgia Conferences.
56. Ibid.
57. Ibid.
58. Ibid.
59. *Southern Christian Advocate* (29 January 1869).
60. *Southern Christian Advocate* (13 November 1868).
61. *Memphis Daily Avalanche* (7 May 1870).
62. Ibid.
63. Ibid.
64. *Journal of the General Conference of the Methodist Episcopal Church, South,* May 1870.
65. Ibid.
66. *Southern Christian Advocate* (16 September 1870).
67. *Southern Christian Advocate* (17 June 1870).
68. Ibid.
69. Othal Hawthorne Lakey, *The History of the CME Church* (Memphis: The CME Publishing House, 1985), 207.
70. Ibid.
71. Ibid.

72. Ibid.

73. W. E. B. DuBois, *The Souls of Black Folk: Essays and Sketches* (New York: Blue Heron Press, 1953), 3.

74. C. H. Phillips, *The History of the Colored Methodist Episcopal Church in America* (Jackson, Tenn.: Publishing House of the CME Church, 1925), 45-46.

75. *Southern Christian Advocate* (4 January 1871).

76. Ibid.

77. J. Jefferson Cleveland and Verolga Nix, ed., *Songs of Zion* (Nashville: Abingdon Press, 1979), 100-101.

78. *Nashville Christian Advocate* (17 January 1877).

79. Isaac Lane, *Autobiography of Bishop Isaac Lane, L.L.D., with a Short History of the C.M.E. Church in America and Methodism* (Nashville: Publishing House of the Methodist Episcopal Church, South, 1916), 98.

80. Ibid.

81. Eula Wallace Harris and Maxie Harris Craig, *Christian Methodist Episcopal Church Through the Years* (Jackson, Tenn.: Christian Methodist Episcopal Church Publishing House, 1948), 17.

82. Phillips, *History of the CME Church in America,* 51.

83. The eminent scholar W. E. B. DuBois predicted at the beginning of the last century that "the problem of the twentieth century is the problem of the color-line" (*On Sociology and Black Community* [Chicago: University of Chicago Press, 1964], 28). With less than a decade remaining in the twentieth century, John Hope Franklin affirmed DuBois's prophecy: "This is the most color-conscious society on the face of the earth. . . . Those who claim [otherwise] . . . merely are ignoring the realities of today. We count everything by race." See *Atlanta Journal / The Atlanta Constitution,* Sunday, July 16, 1995.

84. *Minutes of the Annual Conference of the Methodist Episcopal Church, 1859,* 100.

85. *Minutes, 1866,* 26.

86. Ibid.

87. Ibid., 62.

88. Ibid., 66.

89. Harris and Craig, *Christian Methodist Episcopal Church Through the Years,* 17.

90. Ibid., 18.

91. Elizabeth Beebe, *History and Last Sermon of the Late Bishop Joseph A. Beebe,* 1.

92. Ibid.

93. Ibid.

94. Ibid.

95. Lane, *Autobiography,* 48.

96. Ibid.

97. Ibid.

98. Ibid.

99. Ibid.

100. Lakey, *History of the CME Church,* 148.

101. Lane, *Autobiography,* 48.

102. *Southern Christian Advocate* (13 November 1868).

103. Ibid.

104. *Southern Christian Advocate* (4 May 1866).

105. Stephen Ward Angell, *Bishop Henry McNeal Turner and African-American Religion in the South* (Knoxville: University of Tennessee Press, 1991), 11.

106. Ibid., 12.

107. Holsey, *Autobiography,* 26.

108. Ibid.

109. Ibid.

110. Ibid.

111. Ibid.

112. Ibid., 18.

113. John David Smith, *An Old Creed for the New South* (Westport, Conn.: Greenwood Press, 1985), 206.

114. Holsey, *Autobiography,* 14.

115. Ibid., 19-20.

116. Ibid.

117. John Brother Cade, *Holsey—The Incomparable* (New York: Pageant Press, 1963), 50, 57.

118. Adele Logan Alexander, *Ambiguous Lives: Free Women of Color in Rural Georgia, 1789–1879* (Fayetteville: University of Arkansas Press, 1991), 161.

119. Ibid.

120. Ibid.

121. Ibid., 162.

SELECTED BIBLIOGRAPHY

BOOKS

Adeney, Walter F. *The Greek and Eastern Churches*. Clifton, N.J.: Reference Book Publishers, 1965.

Ahlstrom, Sydney E. *A Religious History of the American People*. New Haven: Yale University Press, 1972.

Alexander, Adele Logan. *Ambiguous Lives: Free Women of Color in Rural Georgia, 1789–1879*. Fayetteville: University of Arkansas Press, 1991.

Alho, Olli. *The Religion of the Slaves: A Study of the Religious Tradition and Behavior of Plantation Slaves in the United States, 1830–1865*. Helsinki: Academia Scientiarum Fennica, 1976.

Ardrey, Robert. *African Genesis*. London: Collins, 1961.

Ayer, Joseph Cullen. *A Source Book for Ancient Church History, from the Apostolic Age to the Close of the Conciliar Period*. New York: Charles Scribner's Sons, 1913.

Baldwin, Lewis V. *"Invisible" Strands in African Methodism: A History of the African Union Methodist Protestant and Union American Methodist Episcopal Churches, 1805–1980*. Metuchen, N.J.: Scarecrow Press, 1983.

Bardolph, Richard. *The Negro Vanguard*. New York: Rinehart, 1959.

Barnes, Albert. *The Antislavery Impulse, 1830–1844*. New York: D. Appleton-Century Co., 1933.

Barnes, Timothy David. *Tertullian: A Historical and Literary Study*. Oxford: Clarendon Press, 1971.

Baur, John. *2000 Years of Christianity in Africa: An African History, 62–1992*. Nairobi, Kenya: Paulines Publication, 1994.

Benjamin, Walter W. "The Era of Reconstruction: The Freemen's Aid

Society." In *The History of American Methodism*, vol. 2, ed. Emory Stevens Burke. New York: Abingdon Press, 1964.

Bennett, Lerone. *Before the Mayflower: A History of the Negro in America, 1619–1966.* Chicago: Johnson Publishing Co, 1966.

Berlin, Ira. *Slaves Without Masters: The Free Negro in the Antebellum South.* New York: Pantheon Books, 1975.

Berry, Mary Francis, and John W. Blassingame. *Long Memory: The Black Experience in America.* New York: Oxford University Press, 1982.

Bettenson, Henry Scowcroft, ed. *Documents of the Christian Church.* 2nd ed. London: Oxford University Press, 1963.

Betts, Albert Deems. *History of South Carolina Methodism.* Columbia, S.C.: Advocate Press, 1952.

Blassingame, John W. *The Slave Community: Plantation Life in the Antebellum South.* New York: Oxford University Press, 1972.

Blassingame, John W., ed. *Slave Testimony: Two Centuries of Letters, Speeches, Interviews, and Autobiographies.* Baton Rouge: Louisiana State University Press, 1977.

Blyden, Edward W. *Christianity, Islam and the Negro Race.* Edinburgh: University Press, 1967.

Boyd, Paul C. *The African Origin of Christianity.* Vol. 1. London: Karea Press, 1991.

Brown, Peter, and Robert Lamont. *Augustine of Hippo: A Biography.* Berkeley: University of California Press, 1967.

Brown, William Wells. *Narrative of William Wells Brown, A Fugitive Slave.* Boston: The Anti-Slavery Office, 1847.

_____. *The Black Man, His Antecedents, His Genius, and His Achievements.* 4th ed. Boston: R. F. Wallcut, 1865.

Bruner, Clarence V. "Religious Instruction of the Slaves in the Antebellum South." Ph.D. diss., Nashville: George Peabody College for Teachers, 1933.

Bury, J. B. *The Invasion of Europe by the Barbarians.* New York: Russell & Russell, 1963.

Cade, John Brother. *Holsey—The Incomparable.* New York: Pageant Press, 1964.

Cannon, James. *History of Southern Methodist Missions.* Nashville: Cokesbury Press, 1926.

Capers, William. *Catechism for the Use of the Methodist Missions.* Nashville: Southern Methodist Publishing House, 1880.

Cash, W. J. *The Mind of the South.* New York: A. A. Knopf, 1941.

Chadwick, Henry. *The Early Church.* London: Hodder & Stoughton, 1968.

Clark, Elmer Talmage. *The Negro and His Religion.* Nashville: Cokesbury Press, 1924.

Coan, Josephus R., and Daniel Alexander Payne. *Christian Educator.* Philadelphia: A.M.E. Book Concern, 1735.

Coleman, Will. *Tribal Talk: Black Theology, Hermeneutics, and African/American Ways of "Telling the Story."* University Park: Pennsylvania State University Press, 2000.

Costen, Melva Wilson. *African American Christian Worship.* Nashville: Abingdon Press, 1993.

Coulter, E. Merton. *The South During Reconstruction, 1865–1877.* Baton Rouge: Louisiana State University Press, 1947.

Courlander, Harold. *The Life and Lore of Haitian People.* Los Angeles: University of California Press, 1973.

Cruden, Robert. *The Negro in Reconstruction.* Englewood Cliffs, N.J.: Prentice-Hall, 1969.

Crum, Mason. *Gullah: Negro Life in the Carolina Sea Islands.* Durham, N.C.: Duke University Press, 1940.

Culver, Dwight W. *Negro Segregation in the Methodist Church.* New Haven, Conn.: Yale University Press, 1953.

Curry, John W. *Passionate Journey: History of the 1866 South Carolina Annual Conference.* Matthew, S.C.: State Printing Company, 1980.

Curtin, Philip D. *The Atlantic Slave Trade: A Census.* Madison: University of Wisconsin Press, 1969.

Curtin, Philip D., ed. *Africa Remembered: Narratives by West Africans from the Era of the Slave Trade.* Madison: University of Wisconsin Press, 1967.

Danquah, J. B. *The African Doctrine of God.* London: Frank Cars and Company, 1968.

Davidson, Basil. *The African Slave Trade.* Rev. and expanded ed. Boston: Little, Brown and Co., 1980.

_____. *The Lost Cities of Africa.* Boston: Little, Brown and Co., 1959.

_____. *The Years of the African Slave Trade.* Boston: Little, Brown and Co., 1961.

Davies, Samuel. *The State of Religion among the Protestant Dissenters in Virginia.* Boston: S. Kneeland, 1751.

Davis, David Brion. *The Problem of Slavery in Western Culture.* Ithaca, N.Y.: Cornell University Press, 1966.

Dill, Samuel. *Roman Society from Nero to Marcus Aurelius.* 2nd ed. New York: Macmillan, 1905.

Diop, Cheikh Anta. *The African Origin of Civilization: Myth or Reality.* New York: L. Hill, 1974.

Dollard, John. *Caste and Class in a Southern Town.* 3rd ed. Garden City, N.J.: Doubleday, 1957.

Drake, St. Clair. *Black Folk Here and There: An Essay in History and Anthropology.* Los Angeles: Center for Afro-American Studies, University of California, 1987–1990.

DuBois, W. E. B. *Africa, Its Geography, People, and Products, and Africa, Its Place in Modern History.* Millwood, N.Y.: KTO Press, 1977.

_____. *Black Reconstruction in America: An Essay Toward a History of the Part Which Black Folk Played in the Attempt to Reconstruct Democracy in America, 1860–1880.* New York: Russell & Russell, 1966.

_____. *The Negro Church.* Atlanta: Atlanta University Press, 1903.

_____. *On Sociology and the Black Community.* Chicago: University of Chicago Press, 1964.

_____. *The Souls of Black Folk.* Greenwich, Conn.: Fawcett Publications, 1961.

_____. *The Suppression of the African Slave Trade to the United States, 1638–1870.* New York: Longman's Green, 1896.

Dumond, Joseph B. *Antislavery: The Crusade for Freedom in America.* Ann Arbor: University of Michigan Press, 1961.

Earl, Riggins Renal. *Dark Symbols, Obscure Signs: God, Self, and Community in the Slave Mind.* Maryknoll, N.Y.: Orbis Books, 1993.

Edwards, Jonathan. *Thoughts on the Revival of Religion in New England.* New York: American Tract Society, 1881.

Eighmy, John Lee. *Churches in Cultural Captivity: A History of the Social Attitudes of Southern Baptists.* Knoxville: University of Tennessee Press, 1987.

Escott, Paul D. *Slavery Remembered: A Record of Twentieth-Century*

Slave Narratives. Chapel Hill: University of North Carolina Press, 1979.

Fage, J. D., and Roland Oliver, eds. *The Cambridge History of Africa.* Vol. 4. New York: Cambridge University Press, 1975–1986.

Farish, Hunter D. *The Circuit Rider Dismounts: A Social History of Southern Methodism, 1865-1900.* Richmond, Va.: Dietz Press, 1938.

Ferris, William R. "The Negro Conversion." *Keystone Folklore Quarterly* (spring 1970): 35-51.

Fickling, Susan Markey. *Slave Conversion in South Carolina, 1830–1860.* Columbia: University of South Carolina, 1924.

Fisher, Miles Mark. *Negro Slave Songs in the United States.* Ithaca, N.Y.: Cornell University Press for the Historical American Association, 1953.

Fleming, Walter L. *Documentary History of Reconstruction.* Vol. 2. New York: McGraw-Hill, 1966.

Foner, Eric. *Nothing but Freedom: Emancipation and Its Legacy.* Baton Rouge: Louisiana State University Press, 1983.

_____. *Reconstruction: America's Unfinished Revolution, 1863–1877.* New York: Harper & Row, 1988.

Foster, Charles I. *An Errand of Mercy: The Evangelical United Front, 1790–1837.* Chapel Hill: University of North Carolina Press, 1960.

Fowler, Warde W. *The Religious Experience of the Roman People, from the Earliest Times to the Age of Augustus.* New York: Cooper Square Publishers, 1971.

Franklin, John Hope. *From Slavery to Freedom: A History of African Americans.* 8th ed. Boston: McGraw-Hill, 2000.

Frazier, E. Franklin. *The Negro Church in America.* New York: Schocken Books, 1964.

Frend, W. H. C. *Martyrdom and Persecution in the Early Church: A Study of a Conflict from the Maccabees to Donatus.* Oxford: Blackwell, 1965.

Frey, Sylvia R., and Betty Wood. *Come Shouting to Zion: African American Protestantism in the American South and British Caribbean to 1830.* Chapel Hill: University of North Carolina Press, 1998.

Gallagher, Buell Gordon. *Color and Conscience: The Irresistible Conflict.* New York: Harper & Brothers, 1946.

Genovese, Eugene D. *Roll, Jordan, Roll: The World the Slaves Made.* New York: Vintage Books, 1976.

George, Carol V. R. *Segregated Sabbaths: Richard Allen and the Emergence of Independent Black Churches, 1760–1840.* New York: Oxford University Press, 1973.

Glover, T. R., trans. *Tertullian, Apology, De Spectaculis, with an English Translation.* New York: G. P. Putnam's Sons, 1931.

Godwin, Morgan. *The Negroes and Indian Advocate.* London: 1680.

Goen, C. C. *Broken Churches, Broken Nation: Denominational Schisms and the Coming of the American Civil War.* Macon, Ga.: Mercer University Press, 1985.

González, Justo. L. *The Story of Christianity.* Vol. 11. San Francisco: Harper & Row, 1984.

Gray, Richard. *The Cambridge Story of Africa.* Vol. 4. New York: Cambridge University Press, 1982.

Greenslade, S. L. *Church and State from Constantine to Theodosius.* Westport, Conn.: Greenwood Press, 1981.

Griaule, Marcel. *Conversation with Ogotemmêli.* London: International African Institute by Oxford University Press, 1965.

Gronniosaw, James Albert Ukawsaw. A *Narrative of the Most Remarkable Particulars in the Life of James Albert Ukawsaw Gronniosaw, An African Prince.* Glascow: David Robertson, Tronsgate, 1840.

Gutman, Herbert G. *The Black Family in Slavery and Freedom, 1750–1925.* New York: Pantheon Books, 1976.

Hagood, Lewis Marshall. *The Colored Man in the Methodist Episcopal Church.* Cincinnati: Cranston & Stowe, 1890.

Harding, Vincent. *There Is a River: The Black Struggle for Freedom in America.* New York: Harcourt Brace Jovanovich, 1981.

Harlan, Howard H. *John Jasper—A Case History in Leadership.* Charlottesville: University of Virginia Press, 1936.

Harnack, Adolf. *The Mission and Expansion of Christianity in the First Three Centuries.* New York: G. P. Putnam's Sons, 1908.

Harris, Joesph E. *Africans and Their History.* New York: Meridian, 1998.

Harris, William C. "James Lynch: Black Leaders in Southern Reconstruction." *The Historian* 34 (November 1971).

Harrison, William Pope. *Gospel among the Slaves*. Nashville: Publishing House of the Methodist Episcopal Church, South, 1893.

Haygood, Atticus G. *Our Brother in Black: His Freedom and His Future*. Freeport, N.Y.: Books for Libraries Press, 1970.

Helps, Arthur. *Life of Las Casas, the Apostle of the Indies*. London: G. Bell and Sons, 1896.

Hening, William Waller. *The Statutes at Large; Being a Collection of All the Laws of Virginia*. Charlottesville: Jamestown Foundation of the Commonwealth of Virginia by the University Press of Virginia, 1969.

Herskovits, Melville J. *The Myth of the Negro Past*. Boston: Beacon Press, 1958.

Hildebrand, Reginald F. *The Times Were Strange and Stirring: Methodist Preachers and the Crisis of Emancipation*. Durham, N.C.: Duke University Press, 1995.

Hilderbrandt, Jonathan. *History of the Church in Africa: A Survey*. Achimota, Ghana, West Africa: Africa Christian Press, 1987.

Hinks, Peter P., ed., *David Walker's Appeal*. University Park: Pennsylvania State University Press, 2000.

Holloway, Joseph E., ed. *Africanisms in American Culture*. Bloomington: Indiana University Press, 1990.

Holme, L. R. *The Extinction of the Christian Churches in North Africa*. New York: B. Franklin, 1969.

Hood, James Walker. *One Hundred Years of the African Methodist Episcopal Zion Church; Or, The Centennial of African Methodism*. New York: A.M.E. Zion Book Concern, 1895.

Hood, Robert E. *Begrimed and Black: Christian Traditions on Blacks and Blackness*. Minneapolis, Minn.: Augsburg Fortress Press, 1994.

Hopkins, Dwight N. *Shoes That Fit Our Feet: Sources for a Constructive Black Theology*. Maryknoll, N.Y.: Orbis Books, 1993.

Hopkins, Dwight N., and George C. L. Cummings, eds. *Cut Loose Your Stammering Tongue: Black Theology in the Slave Narratives*. Maryknoll, N.Y.: Orbis Books, 1991.

Hudson, Winthrop S. *Religion in America*. New York: Scribner's, 1965.

Hurston, Zora Neale. *The Sanctified Church*. Berkeley, Calif.: Turtle Island, 1983.

Idowu, E. Bolaji. *Olodumare: God in Yoruba Belief*. New York: Wazobia, 1994.

Isichei, Elizabeth. *A History of Christianity in Africa: From Antiquity to the Present.* Grand Rapids, Mich.: William B. Eerdmans, 1995.

Jackson, George Pullen. *White and Negro Spirituals, Their Life Span and Kinship: Tracing 200 Years of Untrammeled Song Making and Singing among Our Country Folk.* New York: Da Capo Press, 1975.

James, William. *The Varieties of Religious Experiences.* New York: Vintage Books, 1990.

Jernigan, Marcus W. *Laboring and Dependent Classes in Colonial America, 1607–1783.* Westport, Conn.: Greenwood Press, 1980.

Johnson, Alonzo, and Paul Jersild. *Ain't Gonna Lay My 'Ligion Down: African American Religion in the South.* Columbia, S.C.: University of South Carolina Press, 1996.

Johnson, Charles A. *The Frontier Camp Meeting: Religion's Harvest Time.* Dallas: Southern Methodist University Press, 1955.

Johnson, Clifton, ed. *God Struck Me Dead: Religious Conversion Experiences and Autobiographies of Ex-Slaves.* Philadelphia: Pilgrim Press, 1969.

Johnson, Guy B. *Folk Culture on St. Helena Island, South Carolina.* Hotboro, Pa.: Folklore Associates, 1968.

Johnson, James Weldon. *Along This Way: The Autobiography of James Weldon Johnson.* New York: Da Capo Press, 1973.

Johnson, Joseph A., Jr. *The Soul of the Black Preacher.* Philadelphia: Pilgrim Press, 1971.

Jones, Charles Colcock. *The Religious Instruction of the Negroes in the United States.* Freeport, N.Y.: Books for Libraries Press, 1971.

Jones, Eldred D. *Othello's Countrymen: The African in English Renaissance Drama.* London: Oxford University Press, 1965.

Jordan, Winthrop D. *The White Man's Burden: Historical Origin of Racism in the United States.* New York: Oxford University Press, 1974.

———. *White Over Black: American Attitudes Toward the Negro, 1550–1812.* Chapel Hill: University of North Carolina Press, 1968.

Keller, Charles Roy. *The Second Great Awakening in Connecticut.* New Haven, Conn.: Yale University Press, 1942.

Kidd, B. J. *A History of the Church to* A.D. *461.* 3 Vols. Oxford: Clarendon Press, 1922.

Klein, Herbert S. *Slavery in the Americas: A Comparative Study of Virginia and Cuba*. Chicago: University of Chicago Press, 1967.

Klingberg, Frank J. *An Appraisal of the Negro in Colonial South Carolina: A Study in Americanization*. Washington, D.C.: Associated Publishers, 1941.

Lakey, Othal Hawthorne. *The History of the CME Church*. Memphis: CME Publishing House, 1985.

Lane, Isaac. *Autobiography of Bishop Isaac Lane, L.L.D., with a Short History of the C.M.E. Church in America and of Methodism*. Nashville: Publishing House of the Methodist Episcopal Church, South, 1916.

Latourette, Kenneth Scott. *A History of the Expansion of Christianity*. Vol. 4: *The Great Century in Europe and the United States of America, A.D. 1800–A.D. 1914*. New York: Harper & Brothers, 1937–1945.

Lincoln, C. Eric. *The Black Church Since Frazier*. New York: Schocken Books, 1974.

Mann, Harold W. *Atticus Greene Haygood*. Athens: University of Georgia Press, 1965.

Mannix, Daniel P. *Black Cargoes: A History of the Atlantic Slave Trade, 1518–1865*. New York: Viking Press, 1962.

Martin, Sandy Dwayne. *Black Baptists and African Missions: The Origins of a Movement, 1880–1915*. Macon, Ga.: Mercer University Press, 1989.

Mathews, Donald G. *Religion in the Old South*. Chicago: University of Chicago Press, 1977.

_____. *Slavery and Methodism: A Chapter in American Morality, 1780–1845*. Princeton, N.J.: Princeton University Press, 1965.

Matlack, Lucius C. *Narrative of the Anti-Slavery Experience of a Minister in the Methodist Episcopal Church*. Philadelphia: Merrihew & Thompson, 1845.

Maxson, Charles Hartshorn. *The Great Awakening in the Middle Colonies*. Chicago: University of Chicago Press, 1920.

Mays, Benjamin Elijah. *The Negroe's God as Reflected in His Literature*. Boston: Chapman & Grimes, 1938.

Mays, Benjamin Elijah, and Joseph William Nicholson. *The Negro's Church*. New York: Arno Press, 1969.

Mbiti, John S. *African Religions and Philosophy.* 2nd rev. and enlarged ed. Oxford: Heinemann, 1990.

McCall, Emmanuel L., comp. *The Black Christian Experience.* Nashville: Broadman Press, 1972.

McClain, William B. *Black People in the Methodist Church: Whither Thou Goest?* Cambridge, Mass.: Schenkman Publishing, 1984.

McEvedy, Colin. *The Penguin Atlas of African History.* New York: Penguin Books, 1995.

Mead, Sidney E. *The Lively Experiment: The Shaping of Christianity in America.* New York: Harper & Row, 1963.

Mellon, James, ed. *Bullwhip Days: The Slaves Remember.* New York: Weidenfeld & Nicholson, 1988.

Merdinger, J. E. *Rome and the African Church in the Time of Augustine.* New Haven: Yale University Press, 1997.

Miller, Perry. *Errand into the Wilderness.* Cambridge, Mass.: Belknap Press of Harvard University Press, 1956.

_____. *The Life of the Mind in America, from the Revolution to the Civil War.* New York: Harcourt, Brace and World, 1965.

Mitchell, Henry H. *Black Belief: Folk Beliefs of Blacks in America and West Africa.* New York: Harper & Row, 1975.

_____. *Black Preaching.* Philadelphia: Lippincott, 1970.

Mocko, George Paul. "The Faith of American Slaves, 1830–1860." S.T.M. thesis, Lutheran Theological Seminary, Gettysburg, Pa., 1971.

Montgomery, William E. *Under Their Own Vine and Fig Tree: The African-American Church in the South, 1865–1900.* Baton Rouge: Louisiana State University Press, 1993.

Moore, John Jamison. *History of the AME Zion Church in America: Founded in 1796, in the City of New York.* York, Pa.: Teacher's Journal Office, 1884.

Moorehouse, Henry L. *Baptist Home Missions in America.* New York: Temple Court, 1883.

Morrow, Ralph Ernest. *Northern Methodism and Reconstruction.* East Lansing, Mich.: Michigan State University Press, 1956.

Myerson, Michael. *Nothing Could Be Finer.* New York: International Publishers, 1978.

Nelson, Hart M., Raytha L. Yokley, and Anne K. Nelsen, eds. *The Black Church in America.* New York: Basic Books, 1971.

Neve, J. L. *History of Christian Thought.* Vol. 1. Philadelphia: The United Lutheran Publication House, 1943–1946.

Nichols, Charles H. *Many Thousand Gone: The Ex-Slaves' Account of Their Bondage and Freedom.* Leiden, Netherlands: Brill, 1963.

Niebuhr, H. Richard. *The Kingdom of God in America.* Chicago: Willett, Clark & Co., 1937.

Noble, W. F. P. *A Century of Gospel-work: A History of the Growth of Evangelical Religion in the United States.* Philadelphia: H. C. Watts & Co., 1877.

Norwood, John Nelson. *The Schism in the Methodist Episcopal Church, 1844: A Study of Slavery and Ecclesiastical Politics.* Alfred, N.Y.: Alfred University Press, 1923.

Oates, Stephen B. *Let the Trumpet Sound: The Life of Martin Luther King, Jr.* New York: Harper & Row, 1982.

Offley, G. W. *A Narrative of the Life and Labor of Reverend G. W. Offley, a Colored Man and Local Preacher.* Hartford, Conn.: 1860.

Pamphile, Eusebius. *Ecclesiastical History.* Washington, D.C.: The Catholic University Press, 1955.

Paris, Arthur. *Black Pentecostalism: Southern Religion in an Urban World.* Amherst: University of Massachusetts Press, 1982.

Parish, Peter J. *Slavery: A History and Historians.* New York: Harper & Row, 1989.

Parrinder, Geoffrey. *African Traditional Religion.* Westport, Conn.: Greenwood Press, 1976.

_____. *West African Philosophy.* London: Lutherworth Press, 1951.

Patterson, Caleb Perry. *The Negro in Tennessee, 1790–1865.* Austin, Tex.: University of Texas Press, 1922.

Patterson, Orlando. *Slavery and Social Death: A Comparative Study.* Cambridge, Mass.: Harvard University Press, 1982.

Pettigrew, M. C. *From Miles to Johnson.* Memphis: C.M.E. Church Publishing House, 1970.

Phillips, Charles Henry. *From the Farm to the Bishopric: An Autobiography.* Nashville: Parthenon Press, 1932.

_____. *The History of the Colored Methodist Episcopal Church in America: Comprising Its Organization, Subsequent Development,*

145

and Present Status. Jackson, Tenn.: Publishing House of the C.M.E. Church, 1898.

Phillips, Ulrich B. *American Negro Slavery: A Survey of the Supply, Employment, and Control of Negro Labor as Determined by the Plantation Regime.* Baton Rouge: Louisiana State University Press, 1966.

Pipes, William Harrison. *Say Amen, Brother! Old-Time Negro Preaching: A Study in American Frustration.* New York: William-Frederick Press, 1951.

Ponton, Mungo M. *Life and Times of Henry M. Turner.* Atlanta: A. B. Caldwell Publishing Company, 1917.

Porter, Dorothy B. *Early Negro Writings, 1760–1837.* Boston: Beacon Press, 1971.

Posey, Walter Brownlow. *The Development of Methodism in the Old Southwest, 1783–1824.* Philadelphia: Porcupine Press, 1974.

_____. *Frontier Mission.* Lexington: University of Kentucky Press, 1966.

Purifoy, Lewis M, Jr., "The Methodist-Episcopal Church, South and Slavery, 1844–1865." Ph.D. diss., University of North Carolina, 1965.

Qualben, Lars P. *A History of the Christian Church.* New York: Thomas Nelson, 1936.

Quarles, Benjamin. *Black Abolitionists.* New York: Da Capo Press, 1991.

Raboteau, Albert J. *A Fire in the Bones: Reflections on African-American Religious History.* Boston: Beacon Press, 1995.

_____. *Slave Religion: The "Invisible Institution" in the Antebellum South.* New York: Oxford University Press, 1978.

Ray, Benjamin. *The Encyclopedia of Religion.* New York: Macmillan, 1986.

Redford, A. H. *History of the Organization of the Methodist Episcopal Church, South.* Nashville: Publishing House of the C.M.E. Church, South, 1871.

Reimers, David M. *White Protestantism and the Negro.* New York: Oxford University Press, 1965.

Richardson, Harry Van Buren. *Dark Salvation: The Story of Methodism as It Developed among Blacks in America.* Garden City, N.Y.: Anchor Press, 1976.

Rigell, William Richard. *Negro Religious Leadership in the Southern Seaboard: Maryland, Virginia, North Carolina, South Carolina and Georgia, 1830–1861*. M.A. thesis, University of Chicago Divinity School, 1916.

Rose, Willie Lee. *Rehearsal for Reconstruction: The Port Royal Experiment*. Athens, Ga.: University of Georgia Press, 1999.

Roucek, Joseph, and Thomas Kiernan, eds. *The Negro Impact on Western Civilization*. New York: Philosophical Library, 1970.

Ryder, A. F. C. *Benin and the Europeans: 1485–1877*. New York: Humanities Press, 1969.

Ryland, Garnett. *The Baptists of Virginia, 1699–1926*. Richmond, Va.: Baptist Board of Missions and Education, 1955.

Samkange, Stanlake. *African Saga*. Nashville: Abingdon Press, 1971.

Savage, Horace. *Life and Time of Bishop Isaac Lane*. Nashville: National Publication Co., 1958.

Schaff, Philip. *History of the Christian Church, Nicene and Post-Nicene Christianity from Constantine the Great to Gregory the Great, Vol. III, A.D. 311–600*. Grand Rapids: William B. Eerdmans, 1950.

Schillington, Kevin. *History of Africa*. New York: St. Martin's Press, 1989.

Sernett, Milton C. *Black Religion and American Evangelism*. Metuchen, N.J.: Scarecrow Press, 1975.

Shaw, James Beverly Ford. *The Negro in the History of Methodism*. Nashville: Parthenon Press, 1954.

Shipp, Albert M. *The History of Methodism in South Carolina*. Nashville: Southern Methodist Publishing House, 1884.

Shockley, Grant S., ed. *Heritage and Hope: The African-American Presence in United Methodism*. Nashville: Abingdon Press, 1991.

Shorter, Aylward. *African Christian Spirituality*. Maryknoll, N.Y.: Orbis Books, 1980.

Simms, James M. *The First Colored Baptist Church in North America*. Philadelphia: J. B. Lippincott Company, 1888.

Singleton, George Arnett. "Religious Instruction of the Negro in America Under the Slave Regime." Master's thesis, University of Chicago, 1929.

_____. "The Effect of Slavery Upon the Religion of the Negro." B.D. thesis, University of Chicago Divinity School, 1930.

_____. *The Romance of African Methodism: A Study of the African Methodist Episcopal Church*. New York: Exposition Press, 1952.

Smith, Cortland V. "Church Organization as an Agency of Social Control: Church Discipline in North Carolina, 1800–1860." Ph.D. diss., University of North Carolina, 1966.

Smith, George G. *The Life and Times of George Foster Pierce, with His Sketch of Lovick Pierce, His Father*. Sparta, Ga.: Hancock Publishing Co., 1888.

Smith, H. Shelton. *In His Image, But . . . Racism in Southern Religion, 1780–1910*. Durham, N.C.: Duke University Press, 1972.

Smith, John A. *An Old Creed for the New South: Proslavery Ideology and Historiography, 1865–1914*. Westport, Conn.: Greenwood Press, 1985.

Smith, Timothy L. *Revivalism and Social Reform: American Protestantism on the Eve of the Civil War*. Baltimore: Johns Hopkins University Press, 1980.

Snowden, Frank M. *Blacks in Antiquity: Ethiopians in the Greco-Roman Experience*. Cambridge, Mass.: Belknap Press of Harvard University, 1970.

Sobel, Mechal. *Trabelin' On: The Slave Journal to an Afro-Baptist Faith*. Princeton, N.J.: Princeton University Press, 1988.

Southern, Eileen, ed. *Readings in Black American Music*. New York: W. W. Norton & Co., 1971.

Stampp, Kenneth M. *The Peculiar Institution: Slavery in the Antebellum South*. New York: Vintage Books, 1989.

Staudenraus, P. J. *The African Colonization Movement, 1816–1865*. New York: Octagon Books, 1980.

Stearns, Charles, ed. *Narrative of Henry Box Brown*. Philadelphia: Historic Publications, 1969.

Steward, T. G. *Fifty Years in the Gospel Ministry*. Philadelphia: AME Book Concern, 1930.

Sweet, William Warren. *Religion on the American Frontier: The Baptists, 1783–1830*. New York: Henry Holt & Co., 1931.

_____. *The Story of Religion in America*. New York: Harper and Bros., 1950.

Sydnor, Charles S. *The Development of Southern Sectionalism, 1819–1848*. Baton Rouge: Louisiana State University Press, 1948.

Tannenbaum, Frank. *Slave and Citizen*. Boston: Beacon Press, 1992.

Thomas, Edgar Garfield. *The First African Baptist Church of North America*. Savannah, Ga.: By the Author, 1925.

Thomas, Velma Maia. *Lest We Forget: The Passage from Africa to Slavery and Emancipation*. New York: Crown Trade Paperbacks, 1997.

Thompson, Charles L. *Times of Refreshing: A History of American Revivals from 1740 to 1877, with Their Philosophy and Methods*. Chicago: L. T. Palmer & Co., 1877.

Thompson, H. P. *Into All Lands: History of the Society for the Propagation of the Gospel in Foreign Parts, 1701–1950*. London: SPCK, 1951.

Thornton, John. *Africa and Africans in the Making of the Atlantic World, 1400–1800*. Cambridge: Cambridge University Press, 1998.

Thorpe, Earle E. *The Mind of the Negro: An Intellectual History of Afro-Americans*. Westport, Conn.: Negro Universities Press, 1970.

Thurman, Howard. *Jesus and the Disinherited*. Boston: Beacon Press, 1996.

Tillinghast, Joseph Alexander. *The Negro in Africa and America*. New York: Negro Universities Press, 1968.

Tipple, Ezra S. *Francis Asbury, The Prophet of the Long Road*. New York: Methodist Book Concern, 1916.

Toppin, Edgar A. *A Biographical History of Blacks in America Since 1528*. New York: McKay, 1971.

Toynbee, Arnold. *The Study of History*. New and rev. ed. New York: Weathervane Books, 1972.

Trevor-Roper, Hugh. *The Rise of Christian Europe*. Great Britain: Thames and Hudson, 1965.

Tyms, James D. *The Rise of Religious Education among Negro Baptists: A Historical Case Study*. New York: Exposition Press, 1965.

Wade, Richard C. *Slavery in the Cities: The South, 1820–1860*. New York: Oxford University Press, 1967.

Walker, Clarence E. *A Rock in a Weary Land: The African Methodist Episcopal Church During the Civil War and Reconstruction*. Baton Rouge: Louisiana State University Press, 1982.

Walker, David. *David Walker's Appeal*. New York: Hill and Wang, 1965.

Warmington, B. H. *The North African Provinces from Diocletian to the Vandal Conquest.* Westport, Conn.: Greenwood Press, 1971.

Washington, James M. *Frustrated Fellowship: The Black Baptist Quest for Social Power.* Macon, Ga.: Mercer University Press, 1986.

Washington, Joseph R., Jr. *Black Religion: The Negro and Christianity in the United States.* Lanham, Md.: University Press of America, 1984.

Weatherford, Willis Duke. *American Churches and the Negro: An Historical Study from Early Slave Days to the Present.* Boston: Christopher Publishing House, 1957.

_____. *The Negro from Africa to America.* Boston: Christopher Publishing House, 1957.

Weeks, Stephen B. *Southern Quakers and Slavery: A Study of Institutional Slavery.* New York: Bergman Publishers, 1968.

Weisberger, Bernard A. *They Gathered at the River: The Story of the Great Revivalists and Their Impact upon Religion in America.* New York: Octagon Books, 1979.

Whitehead, Alfred North. *Adventures of Ideas.* New York: Macmillan, 1955.

Whitham, A. R. *The History of the Christian Church.* London: Rivingtons, 1936.

Wilken, Robert L. *The Christians as the Romans Saw Them.* New Haven: Yale University Press, 1984.

Williams, George W. *History of the Negro Race in America from 1619 to 1880.* New York: G. P. Putnam's Sons, 1882.

Williams, Thomas Leonard. "The Methodist Mission to the Slaves." Ph.D. diss., Yale University, 1943.

Williamson, Joel. *After Slavery: The Negro in South Carolina During Reconstruction, 1861–1877.* Hanover, N.H.: University Press of New England, 1990.

Wilmore, Gayraud S. *Black Religion and Black Radicalism: An Interpretation of the Religious History of African Americans.* Maryknoll, N.Y.: Orbis Books, 1998.

Wimberly, Edward P., and Anne S. Wimberly. *Liberation and Human Wholeness: The Conversion Experiences of Black People in Slavery and Freedom.* Nashville: Abingdon Press, 1986.

Winks, Robin W. *The Blacks in Canada: A History.* Montreal: McGill-Queens University, 1997.

Wojcikowski, Jennifer Judith. "Negotiating Ecclesiastical Identity: Black Southern Methodism and the Creation of the Colored Methodist Episcopal Church in America, 1866–1870." Master's thesis, University of North Carolina, 1994.

Wood, Forrest G. *The Arrogance of Faith: Christianity and Race in America from the Colonial Era to the Twentieth Century.* New York: Alfred A. Knopf, 1990.

Wood, Peter H. *Black Majority: Negroes in Colonial South Carolina from 1670 Through the Stono Rebellion.* New York: Alfred A. Knopf, 1974.

Woodson, Carter G. *The African Background Outlined, Or, Handbook for the Study of the Negro.* New York: Negro Universities Press, 1968.

_____. *The Education of the Negro Prior to 1861: A History of the Education of the Colored People of the United States from the Beginning of Slavery to the Civil War.* New York: G. P. Putnam's Sons, 1915.

_____. *The History of the Negro Church.* Washington, D.C.: Associated Publishers, 1921.

Wright, Luis B. *Culture on the Moving Frontier.* Bloomington, Ind.: Indiana University Press, 1955.

ARTICLES, JOURNALS, AND MINUTES

Askew, Glenn T. "Black Elitism and the Failure of Paternalism in Post-Bellum Georgia: The Case of Bishop Lucius Henry Holsey." *The Journal of Southern History* 58 (4 November 1992).

Atlanta Journal Constitution, 31 December 1994–2 July 1995.

Atlantic Monthly. "Insight, the Negro Power of Perception." (September 1938).

Bailey, Kenneth K. "The Post Civil War Racial Separations in Southern Protestantism: Another Look." *Church History* 46 (December 1977).

_____. "Protestant and Afro-Americans in the Old South: Another Look." *The Journal of Southern History* 41 (November 1975): 451-72.

Beaufort Gazette, 28 July 1991.

Beebe, Elizabeth. "History and Last Sermon of the Late Joseph A. Beebe." (15 June 1951).

Boston Weekly Newsletter, 21 August 1740.

Christian Advocate, 1866–1871.

The Christian Recorder, 1866–1871.

Colored American (Augusta, Ga.), 1866–1871.

Cross, F. L. "History and Fiction in the African Canons." *Journal of Theological Studies* 12 (1961): 227-47.

Del Pinto, Julius E. "Blacks in the United Methodist Church from Its Beginning to 1968." *Methodist History* 19 (October 1980).

Duke Magazine, November-December 1995.

Durant, Thomas J., Jr. "The Enduring Legacy of the African American Plantation." *The Journal of Negro History* 80, no. 12 (Spring 1995).

Episcopal Address to the General Conference of the Colored Methodist Episcopal Church, 1922.

Ferris, William, Jr., "The Negro Conversion." *Keystone Folklore Quarterly* (Spring 1970): 35-51.

Fickling, Susan Markey. "Slave Conversion in South Carolina: 1830–1860." *Bulletin of the University of South Carolina,* no. 146 (1 September 1924).

Gallay, Allan. "The Origins of Slave Holders' Paternalism: George Whitefield, the Bryan Family and the Great Awakening in South Carolina." *Journal of Southern History* 53, no. 3 (3 August 1987).

General Conference of the Methodist Episcopal Church Minutes, 1965.

Gravely, William B. "A Black Methodist on Reconstruction in Mississippi: Three Letters by James Lynch in 1868–1869." *Methodist History* 18 (October 1979): 3-25.

Harrison, W. P., *The Gospel among the Slaves: A Short Account of Missionary Operation among the African Slaves of the Southern States.* Nashville: Nashville Publishing House of the C.M.E. Church, South, 1893.

Hening, Wilborn W. *Statutes at Large: Being a Collection of All the Laws of Virginia from the First Session of the Legislature in the Year 1619.* Vol. 6. Richmond: Franklin Press, 1891.

Hewalt, Alexander. "An Historical Account of the Rise and Progress of South Carolina and Georgia." London: n.p., 1779, in the Carrol Historical Collection in South Carolina.

Hildebrand, Reginald F. "Methodist Episcopal Policy on the Ordination of Black Minutes, 1784–1864." *Methodist History* 20 (April 1981).

Jackson, Harvey. "The Carolina Connection: Jonathan Bryan, His Brothers and Founding of Georgia, 1733–1752." Beaufort County, S.C.: Historical Society.

_____. "Hugh Bryan and the Evangelical Movement in Colonial South Carolina." *William and Mary Quarterly* 43 (October 1986).

Jackson, L. P. "Religious Development of the Negro in Virginia from 1760–1869." *Journal of Negro History* (1931).

Journal of the General Conference of the Colored Methodist Episcopal Church in America, 1870. Jackson, Tenn.: First M.E. Church, 16-21 December 1870.

Journal of the General Conference of the Methodist Church, 1840.

Journal of the General Conference of the Methodist Episcopal Church, 1844.

Kenny, William A. "Alexander Garden and George Whitefield: The Significance of Revivalism in South Carolina, 1738–1741." *South Carolina Historical Magazine* 71 (June 1970).

Lambert, Frank. "I Saw the Book Talk: Slave Readings of the First Great Awakening." *Journal of Negro History* 77, no. 4 (Summer 1994): 185-98.

Lawrence, James B. "Religious Education of the Negro in the Colony of Georgia." *Georgia Historical Quarterly* 11 (March 1930): 41-57.

Lovell, John, Jr. "The Social Implications of the Negro Spiritual." *Journal of Negro Education* 8 (October 1939): 634-43.

Mathews, Donald G. "The Second Great Awakening as an Organizing Process, 1780–1830: An Hypotheses." *American Quarterly* 21 (Winter 1969): 40.

Memphis Daily Advocate, 7 May 1870.

Minutes of the Annual Conferences of the Methodist Episcopal Church in America. Nashville: First M.E. Church, South, 1870.

Minutes of the Annual Conferences of the Methodist Episcopal Church, South for the Year 1866. Nashville: Southern Methodist Publishing House, 1870.

Minutes of the Annual Conferences of the Methodist Episcopal Church, South. Nashville: Southern Methodist Publishing House, 1860.

Moore, LeRoy. "The Spiritual: Soul of Black Religion." *American Quarterly* 23, no. 5 (1971).

Nashville Christian Advocate, 14 January 1877.

Newman, Harvey K. "Piety and Segregation: White Protestant Attitudes Towards Blacks in Atlanta, 1865–1905." *Georgia Historical Quarterly* (Summer 1979).

Peyton, Green. "Call Me a Confederate." *The Southern Literary Messenger* 1, no. 1 (July 1939).

Raleigh Christian Advocate, 1871.

Raymond, Charles. "The Religious Life of the Negro Slave." *Harper's Magazine* 27 (October 1863).

Southern Christian Advocate, 1865–1871.

Southern Evangelical Intelligencer, 12 and 26 June 1819.

Stevens, Robert. *To the Society for Propagation of the Gospel, N.D.* (November 1785).

Summers, Thomas O., ed. *Journal of the General Conference of the Methodist Episcopal Church, South, 1866–1874.* Nashville: Publishing House of the Methodist Episcopal Church, South, 1866.

Tippie, Azras. *The Heart of Asbury's Journal Being the Substance of the Printed Journals of Reverend Frances Asbury.* New York: Eaton & Mains, 1904.

Tupper, H. H. "History of the First Baptist Church in South Carolina." *Journal of Episcopal Church* (1830).

Wauglean, Alden T. "Blacks in Virginia." *William and Mary Quarterly*, third series, 30 (July 1972).

Whitefield, George. "A Journal of a Voyage from London to Savannah in Georgia." London: W. Straham, 1743.

Wilson, G. R. "The Religion of the American Negro Slave: His Attitude Toward Life and Health." *Journal of Negro History* 8, no. 1 (January 1923).

INDEX

Walker, David, 65, 128n. 4
Walton, George, 54
war, 26
    Civil. *See* Civil War
    Revolutionary. *See* Revolutionary
        War
Washington, Booker T., 116
water, 42
Watson, Samuel, 99, 110
Weems, Jim, 115
Weld, Theodore Dwight, 67-68
Wesley, John, 38-39, 87, 92, 126n. 30
Wesley, Susanna, 38
West, Edward, 98, 101
West Indies, 23-24, 27
Wheatley, Phillis, 61-62, 116
White, William, 85
Whitefield, George, 53, 56, 126n. 31
    and conversion of Marrant, 17-18,
        43

pietism of, 38
Williams, Nancy, 14-15
Williams, Peter, 86
Williams, Robert, 18
Willis, Joseph, 60
Wilson, A. K., 113-14
Wojcikowski, Jennifer Judith, 85
women, 29, 42, 67
Wood, Peter H., 17, 43
Woodman, Charles, 59
Woodson, Carter G., 47
world, transformation of, 68
worship
    demonstrative, 37-38, 59, 77
    gathering, 36-37, 59, 61, 70, 72,
        78-80
Wragg, Betsy, 111
Wragg, Judeth, 111